The Metaverse for Learning and Education

Accompanying *The Metaverse: A Critical Introduction* in CRC Press' new The Metaverse Series, this book explores the ways in which the Metaverse can be used for education and learning, as well as how it is different from virtual reality (VR) application development. For example, institutions and tutors can make use of the Metaverse space to represent themselves in it or create their own content and share experiences, whilst students can access a wider range of material, learn within appropriate settings and create content to support their own and others' learning.

Key Features:

- Provides practical advice from the authors' collective three decades of work and experience in VR and Metaverse learning and education.
- Examines different approaches to learning that are relevant in a VR and Metaverse context, including theoretical and practical approaches to pedagogy.
- Suggests different approaches to learning that might be used and explores learning in practice in the metaverse – from early versions such as computer-supported collaborative learning and action learning through to more recent practices such as games and gamification and the use of problem-based learning in virtual worlds.
- Examines a number of advantages of learning in the metaverse such as the opportunity to be inclusive towards different approaches to learning, the value of affordances, peer-to-peer learning and genres of participation.

This book is aimed primarily at practitioners in the learning and education field, and those who set policy and commission work. It may also be of interest to parents, managers, other interested professionals, students, researchers and lay readers.

The Metaverse Series

The Metaverse: A Critical Introduction
David Burden & Maggi Savin-Baden
A well-grounded introduction to the concept of the Metaverse, its history, the technology, the opportunities, the challenges and how it is having an impact almost every facet of society.

The Metaverse for Learning and Education
Maggi Savin-Baden & David Burden
A clear and concise guide for practitioners and other interested readers in how the Metaverse and related technologies can be best used to create and deliver innovative learning and education, and how the delivery of learning and education in the Metaverse might evolve.

The Metaverse for Psychotherapy: A Practitioner's Guide to Effective Mental Health Treatment
Bruce Bassi
A guide for clinicians and other interested readers in how the Metaverse and related technologies can be best used to deliver effective psychotherapy and how the delivery of psychotherapy in the Metaverse might evolve.

Cities in the Metaverse: Digital Twins, Society, Avatars, and Economics on the New Frontier
Andrew Hudson-Smith, Valerio Signorelli, and Duncan Wilson
Cities in the Metaverse delves into the possibilities and challenges of a future where we can interact with each other in virtual spaces, create digital twins of real-world cities, and even build new worlds based on AI.

The Military Metaverse: The Opportunities and Challenges for Global Security
Andy Fawkes and David Burden
The Military Metaverse explores the impact that the Metaverse is having today on how the world's militaries procure, maintain, train, plan, and fight, and how the Metaverse presents new challenges and potentially even a new environment for future conflicts.

The Metaverse and Religion
Eric Trozzo
The Metaverse and Religion provides a balanced consideration to ways that the Metaverse poses challenges to conventional conceptions of religion, exploring the new understandings of religion that may be opened up, and how it might be used by religious movements.

For more information and further titles in this series please visit:
https://www.routledge.com/The-Metaverse/book-series/

The Metaverse for Learning and Education

Maggi Savin-Baden and David Burden

CRC Press
Taylor & Francis Group
Boca Raton London New York

CRC Press is an imprint of the
Taylor & Francis Group, an **informa** business
A CHAPMAN & HALL BOOK

First edition published 2025
by CRC Press
2385 NW Executive Center Drive, Suite 320, Boca Raton FL 33431

and by CRC Press
4 Park Square, Milton Park, Abingdon, Oxon, OX14 4RN

CRC Press is an imprint of Taylor & Francis Group, LLC

ISBN: 9781032538341 (hbk)
ISBN: 9781032538334 (pbk)
ISBN: 9781003413875 (ebk)

DOI: 10.1201/9781003413875

Typeset in Palatino
by KnowledgeWorks Global Ltd.

To my brother, Mike Savin, a kind

and loving soul.

You are a gift.

Contents

About the Authors

Maggi Savin-Baden is a Research Professor at Blackfriars Hall, University of Oxford. She has researched and evaluated staff and student experience of learning for over 20 years and gained funding. Maggi has a strong publication record of over 70 research publications and has completed 25 books. Her research and writing reflect her interests on the impact of innovative learning, digital fluency, digital afterlife and the postdigital, and she has worked with David on a number of research projects since 2008.

David Burden created his first virtual world in 1996 and has spent most of the time since working in virtual spaces and with virtual humans for a variety of clients through his company Daden Limited. His first presentation on the Metaverse was in 2008. David and Maggi co-wrote the book *Virtual Humans* for Routledge in 2019, and also worked together on the book Digital Afterlife in 2020.

Acknowledgements

This book has been a challenge to create in a changing higher education system and postdigital world.

Our sincerest thanks to Randi Slack at CRC/Taylor and Francis for being so positive when we suggested the idea of not one but a whole series of books on the Metaverse, and who has been so supportive of us both since our initial work on Virtual Humans.

We are grateful to Dave White, senior lecturer in visual communication, University of the Arts, United Kingdom, for permission to use his Visitors and Residents continuum (Figure 4.2).

We are thankful to John Savin-Baden who has critiqued the text and supported the editing process. Any mistakes and errors are ours.

That unknown is a diamond in a universe of dirt. Uncertainty. Unpredictability. It is when you turn your emotions into art. It is BTS and the Sistine Chapel and Rumi's poetry and Ross Geller on the stairs yelling, 'Pivot.' Every creation great and small, they are our diamonds.

(Green, 2020*, p 196)

*Green, H. (2020) A Beautifully Foolish Endeavor. Trapeze p. 196

Introduction

David and I began the journey of exploring the metaverse for learning and education as far back as 2008. It was not called the metaverse then, but we began by exploring the virtual world for learning in higher education. From there, we progressed to exploring the use of chatbots and then virtual humans. The latter resulted in our book on *Virtual Humans* (Burden & Savin-Baden, 2019). Since then, between us, we have examined digital immortality, gaming, war gaming and the postdigital. This text brings together our interest in education and learning that has spanned over 15 years.

The Metaverse for Learning and Education is part of The Metaverse Series and aims to help practitioners to understand the value and implications of the metaverse and related metaverse technologies such as virtual reality technology, in the evolving delivery of learning and education. The *Metaverse for Learning and Education* is aimed primarily at practitioners in the learning and education field, and those who set policy and commission work. It may also be of interest to parents, managers, other interested professionals, students, researchers and lay readers.

It begins with Chapter 1, The metaverse for learning and education, which considers how the metaverse might be delineated, adopted and adapted. This chapter explores what counts as education in the 21st century, locates the metaverse in relation to this and then explores the challenges of learning in the metaverse, issues of embodiment and some of the current claims and concerns about the metaverse for learning and education. From here, Chapter 2, Approaches to learning, provides a detailed examination of the different approaches to learning that are relevant to the metaverse. It begins by discussing learning theories and explores how these may or may not enable effective learning for students. The second section of the chapter examines different types of teaching, from traditional lecture-based learning to more learner-centred approaches, such as problem-based learning and collaborative learning. The final section of the chapter suggests particular modes of learning that may easily be adapted for the metaverse. Chapter 3 builds on this and explores applied models for learning. The main argument of this chapter is that whilst the concept of the metaverse is relatively new in university and college learning spaces, the metaverse and related technology have been in use since the late 1990s and came to prominence with the growth and use of virtual worlds from 2003 onwards. This chapter begins by exploring the shifts from earlier versions, to current versions of the metaverse. It then suggests different approaches to learning that might be used

DOI: 10.1201/9781003413875-1

and explores learning in practice in the metaverse. The approaches vary from early versions, such as computer-supported collaborative learning and action learning, to more recent practices, such as games and gamification and the use of problem-based learning in virtual worlds.

Chapter 4, Rethinking pedagogy for the metaverse, considers the impact of advances in technology on pedagogy and the increasing use of learning online. It begins by examining the stances and experiences of learners in the metaverse, drawing on both older and more recent research. The importance of the stances model of learning is that it offers an alternative view of student learning from the standardized model of learning styles. The chapter then explores some of the particular areas of value when using the metaverse, including the value of the visual, the value of learning spaces, the value of openness and the value of experiential opportunities. The final section of the chapter examines the broader impact of the metaverse on higher education and suggests that pedagogy needs to be re-examined in the light of the metaverse. Building on the broader picture of pedagogy, Chapter 5 then focusses on the details of the tech, platforms and wearables in the postdigital metaverse. This chapter begins by exploring the context of learning in the metaverse for a postdigital age. The postdigital is a term that is seen as both confusing and controversial, but it is a useful concept for explaining the impact of the digital on human and non-human actors. The second section of the chapter examines the tech and the platforms. Whilst many of these have been in use since the 1990s many of these remain in use 25 years later, but there are now newer and more flexible options available. The final section presents new practices such as wearable devices and lifelogging.

The final two chapters of the book explore the challenges of the metaverse and possible futures it may offer. In Chapter 6, Pros and cons of learning in the metaverse, we examine a number of advantages of learning in the metaverse such as the opportunity to be inclusive towards different approaches to learning, the value of affordances, peer-to-peer learning and genres of participation. The second section of the chapter explores some of the challenges of learning in the metaverse. These challenges include digital inequalities and surveillance, the question of virtue ethics, power and control, and mis/placed digital identities. The final chapter, Chapter 7, Learning assemblages for the metaverse, examines the idea of learning assemblages, which reflects changing views of how learning might be seen in the metaverse. It begins by presenting the notion of learning assemblages and illustrating why this is important to the metaverse. The chapter then explores issues that are related to the idea of assemblages, beginning with context and collision collapse and digital métissage. The latter half of the chapter discusses ways of rethinking place, space and presence, suggesting that these concepts are currently defined too narrowly and need to be re-examined in light of future forms of learning in the metaverse.

Through this text, we seek to encourage not only an understanding what constitutes the metaverse, but also a rethinking of what learning and education mean in a postdigital age. The speed of technology and the practicality of our lives never really match one another, but if we can learn to live liquid lives, we believe the metaverse can help us to become innovative critical beings. Universities and businesses need to create new approaches to learning, education and knowledge creation that acknowledge and embrace transformational technologies in ways that are candid, benevolent and combine hope, moral responsibility and politics with a critical edge.

Reference

Burden, D., & Savin-Baden, M. (2019). *Virtual humans: Today and tomorrow.* CRC Press.

1

The Metaverse for Learning and Education

Introduction

The main difficulty with the metaverse is that it is a slippery concept with few boundaries. Since the early 2020s, the term has expanded and grown in use, encompassing a shifting array of technologies and practices. This chapter explores the idea of the Metaverse for learning and education and considers how it might be delineated, adopted and adapted. It begins by exploring what counts as education in the 21st century and locating the metaverse in relation to this. The chapter then explores the challenges of learning in the metaverse, issues of embodiment and some of the current claims and concerns about the metaverse for learning and education.

Education in the 21st Century

The increasing body of knowledge about how students learn has created a move within the higher education system itself to create educational environments which are more conducive to learning. Curriculum design has also been an area of growing interest. However, with issues of increased accountability and government intervention in higher education, along with concerns about plagiarism and the need to ensure students 'pass the programme,' there has been a marked shift towards the use of training and instruction – even though these words may not be used to refer to the practices that take place. This is important in terms of the metaverse because there is a difference between training and learning activities in the metaverse. Training involves acquiring and practising skills, whereas learning is gaining a deep understanding of knowledge and being able to critique it.

The pioneering work of Stenhouse (1975) challenged the use of behavioural methods in the design of curricula. Stenhouse's fundamental objections to the universal application of objectives are that it both mistakes the nature of knowledge and the nature of improving practice. He distinguished between

DOI: 10.1201/9781003413875-2

four different educational processes: training, instruction, initiation and induction, and argued that although the objectives model offers a reasonably good fit between training and instruction, this is not so with initiation and induction. Stenhouse's main focus is that of induction into knowledge since the most important characteristic of this mode is that one can 'think with it': knowledge he argues is a structure to sustain creative thought and provide frameworks for judgment and is largely concerned with synthesis. Hence:

- Training is seen as the acquisition of skills, with the result that successful training is deemed as the capacity for performance.
- Induction involves the introduction of someone into the thought system of the culture and here successful induction would be characterized by a person's ability to develop relationships and judgments in relation to that culture.

His stance still has relevance today:

> The demand for objectives is a demand for justification rather than simply description of ends. As such it is part of a political dialogue rather than an educational one. It is not about curriculum design, but rather an expression of irritation in the face of the problem of accountability in education. I believe that politicians will have to face the fact that there is no easy road to accountability via objectives. Payment by results showed that.
>
> **(Stenhouse, 1975, p. 77)**

Thus education is not the same as training. Training focusses on the learning and acquisition of particular skills, whereas education enables students to consider and critique the knowledge put before them. Education seeks to encourage students to learn, question and see it as a component of life, rather than just equipping them for life and work. These differences are listed in Table 1.1.

TABLE 1.1 Education, Learning and Training in the Metaverse

	Definition	Example	Related Article
Education in the metaverse	The process of receiving knowledge or instruction for a particular purpose.	The use of immersive journalism to educate wide audiences.	de la Peña et al. (2010)
Learning in the metaverse	The process of acquiring, understanding and using knowledge.	Students as co-creators of learning experiences in virtual worlds (VWs).	Mårell-Olsson (2019)
Training in the metaverse	Developing specific skills or behaviours.	Safety training using virtual reality (VR).	Sacks et al. (2013)

The examples mentioned in Table 1.1 are only an initial guide to education, learning and training in the metaverse, and the next section examines in more detail what counts as the metaverse in the 21st century.

Locating the Metaverse

One of the concerns raised by academics and the general public when the subject of the metaverse is discussed is that it is just another component of the relentless change of the 21st century. To some extent, the idea of the metaverse brings with it a feeling of liminality, living in the in-between, and yet too living at the borders and possibilities of something new. There is a sense too, that we are in a space of waiting. The writer and theologian C.S. Lewis (1952) suggested the hall was a waiting room with many doors.

> The hall is a place to wait in, a place from which to try the various doors, not a place to live in. For that purpose the worst of the rooms (whichever that may be), is, I think, preferable. It is true that some people may find they have to wait in the hall for a considerable time, while others feel certain almost at once which door they must knock at. (p. 11)

This, we suggest, is a useful way of imagining the metaverse. Going into a room changes our perspective before we return to the hall; we have a different view. What is challenging in the early 2020s, however, is that halls, doors and perspectives are so different, resulting in the continual question: what is the metaverse and what does it mean for education?

There have been arguments that the metaverse came into being in the early 2000s, or even before, with the educational use of VWs, such as *Second Life*. In the 2000s, the focus tended to be on separate entities, such as a VW, haptics or augmented reality (AR). Yet despite more recent definitions of the metaverse, there are still articles that suggest that VWs such as *Second Life*, games such as *World of Warcraft* and other massively multiplayer online games can still be classed as examples of the metaverse (Tlili et al., 2022). However, we argue that what is different about the use of the metaverse for learning and education in the 2020s is the merging and melding of technologies, platforms and human beings. Burden & Savin-Baden (2019) published a book entitled *Virtual Humans* which began the work of exploring what it means to be a virtual human. Virtual humans are human-like characters that may be seen on a computer screen, heard through a speaker or accessed in some other way. They exhibit human-like behaviours, such as speech, gesture and movement, and might also show other human characteristics, such as emotions, empathy, reasoning, planning, motivation and the development and use of memory. However, a precise definition of what represents a virtual human or even 'artificial intelligence' (AI) is constantly changing. Furthermore, the distinctions between different types of virtual humans, such as a chatbot, conversational agent, autonomous agent or pedagogic agent, are unclear, as well as how virtual humans relate to robots and androids. A virtual human is just one component of the metaverse, as Knox (2022) argues:

> The metaverse is not simply a platform developed by one company, implying the usual constraints of monopolisation, but rather a new plane of existence, not just void of control by any single corporation, but also free of incursions by any state entity or government. In this sense, a generous view of the metaverse would perceive it as a political project, and one that seeks to continue the ideals of independence and frontierism that excited the early protagonists of cyberspace. (p. 210)

Hwang and Chien (2022) suggest that what makes the metaverse different from AR and VR is that it is shared, persistent and decentralized. In practice, they argue that central to the creation of such a metaverse is a nonplayer character (which they term an AI) who is there to provide support, guidance and peer interaction for those using the metaverse. Whilst this is an interesting stance, it does not entirely deal with the complexity of merging technologies, the issues of embodiment and covert concerns such as power and surveillance, which are described in Table 1.2.

TABLE 1.2 Understanding the Metaverse

The Metaverse as	Definition	Related Work
Embodied internet	Suggested by Zuckerberg that it is the idea of being in the experience, not just looking at it.	Chayka (2021)
Collective space	A perpetual shared concurrent 3D virtual space connected with a virtual universe.	Lee et al. (2021)
An internet application	An application that integrates a range of new technologies.	Ning et al. (2021)
Melded technologies	The melding of AR technologies into one unique metaverse.	Parisi (2021)
Post-reality universe	A perpetual and persistent multiuse environment merging digital virtuality with physical reality.	Mystakidis (2022)
Power	Pervasive power that controls social life and social spaces.	Freuler and Cruz (2021)
Surveillance	The use of data shared in digital space to track and trace people's behaviours and habits.	Savin-Baden (2023)

Re/emergence of Transformative Technologies

The abiding idea of transformative technologies is that they transform society and indeed the world in some way. Examples of transformative technologies include early technologies such as the wheel, the contraceptive pill and more recently in vitro fertilization and solar energy. The nature and extent of these particular examples of transformation are still seen as being contentious. Luck and Clarke (2022) argue that transformative technologies should significantly transform the state of affairs, suggesting in fact many have not. Learning through transformative technologies, such as simulations and VWs, has become a component in many curricula. Virtual worlds are three-dimensional graphical online environments, which users can change and manipulate, as well as work simultaneously on specifically tailored or self-developed projects. However, the use of VR remains underused in curricula, particularly in the arts. Yet this a technology that can support and promote creativity in online learning spaces that have become linear and overmanaged and offers the opportunity to consider the oblique function.

Virtual reality is being increasingly used throughout public and private sector organizations to teach and train people at all levels, from teaching history, geography and STEAM subjects in schools and colleges to maintaining equipment, dealing with customers, delivering hospital care and visualizing and experiencing new environments and even new data sets.

As mentioned, in the first book of the series; The Metaverse. A Critical Introduction to the (Burden & Savin-Baden, 2024) one of the difficulties with the emergence and development of the Metaverse is the definition of how it might be constituted and the terms used to define it. An example of this is the concept of extended reality – which might be argued to be the current most accurate definition of the metaverse. Extended reality is the broadest term covering VR, AR and mixed reality (MR). It has been defined as:

> XR or Extended Reality are technologies that create immersive experiences in which users interact with digital content in a digital or virtual reality (VR), that augment reality (AR) allowing users to interact with digital content in the real world, or create various blends where users interact with real or digital content within a mixed reality (MR).
>
> **(Bogan et al., 2019)**

Table 1.3 summarizes the key different forms of extended reality, and each is described in more detail in the following sections.

Virtual Reality

There are a number of definitions of VR, including 'real-time interactive graphics with 3D models, combined with a display technology that gives the

TABLE 1.3 Forms of Extended Reality (based on Burden et al., 2022)

Form of VR	Definition
Virtual reality (VR)	An immersive experience where the user experiences, is immersed in and has agency within a digital, artificial environment (usually primarily visual) which delivers a sense of 'being there,' whilst any physical world awareness is minimized.
Desktop VR	An immersive 3D experience delivered using a conventional 2D computer screen (desktop, laptop, tablet or mobile), in either first or third person where the user can navigate and interact with a rich virtual environment (such as *Fortnite*, *World of Warcraft*, *Second Life*).
Head-mounted display VR (HMD VR)	Virtual reality explicitly delivered through a head-mounted display (HMD), which completely covers the user's field of view, offers 3 or 6 degrees of freedom (3DOF/6DOF) and hand controllers or gesture control.
Augmented reality (AR)	Overlays digital information onto a camera (typically smartphone) viewscreen and thus 'rather than replacing reality, it supplements it' (Azuma, 1997).
Mixed reality (MR)	Overlays digital information onto a head-mounted see-through screen, where the digital information is 'aware' of the physical geometry of the world and responds to it.
Virtual worlds (VWs)	Virtual worlds refer to computer-based, multi-user virtual environments that simulate real or fictional life and that users live and work in through their graphical representations or avatars.

user the immersion in the model world and direct manipulation' (Bishop & Fuchs, 1992). The image of the HMD has become synonymous with the idea of VR. As the name suggests, they attach to the head and present images to the visual system. They are based upon the effective application of numerous technological systems to enable the user to feel 'present' in the VW. In contrast, non-HMDs are largely seen in relation to gaming, gamification and immersive VWs. Virtual Reality headsets can be used in numerous contexts from gaming to healthcare and can be used to facilitate and support training and learning of new skills. Examples include combat training, workplace discrimination training and developing surgical skills in medicine and dentistry. Learning through an immersive VR environment is all-encompassing and eliminates the distractions that might impair learning. Furthermore, the relative novelty (depending on individual experience) is likely to make it more memorable due to the intensity of the experience.

Augmented Reality

Augmented reality is defined as an enhanced version of reality created by the use of technology to overlay digital information on an image of something being viewed through a device. In practice, this takes the real-life environment around us into a digital interface by putting virtual objects in real time, such as Google Maps, where it is possible to see the surrounding environment in 3D. A further example is Sunseeker, an app which provides a flat compass view and a 3D view showing the solar path, its hour intervals, its equinox, winter and summer solstice and a map view showing solar direction for each daylight hour.

Mixed Reality

Mixed reality is the merging of real and virtual worlds to produce new environments and visualizations, where physical and digital objects co-exist and interact in real time.

One example of this is the use of HoloAnatomy (Ruthberg et al., 2020) where the MR platform was used to learn anatomy for cadaveric dissection. The findings indicate that the average study time of 48 medical students who completed study requirements was 4.564 hours using HoloAnatomy and 7.318 hours in the cadaver lab ($p = 0.001$), suggesting HoloAnatomy may decrease the time necessary for anatomy didactics without sacrificing student understanding of the material.

Embodiment and Learning

Embodiment has been discussed extensively in education and computer science. For example, the creation and use of avatars in educational games and VWs have introduced questions about the sense of being embodied, the relationship with the avatar and the challenge of identity construction. There is an interesting juxtaposition of real life and the metaverse and the extent to which one feels more 'real' in spaces such as a VW or AR, than in online discussion forums. There seems to be something about being able to represent oneself visually, being able to make choices about what one looks like and how one can move, that gives a stronger sense of *being* present and learning differently even if one is not face-to-face in a physical space. Perhaps this is related to being able to choose how to represent oneself or to do with feeling more embodied.

Although some years old, Gee's work on video gaming offers some sense of the multiplicity of identities involved in online learning. Gee (2004, pp. 112–113) developed a theory of identity, based on experience of videogaming. It is a tripartite identity comprising:

1. The real identity: who we are in the physical world.
2. The virtual identity: who we are in the virtual space. Thus, Gee argues, our virtual self should be able to 'inherit' some of our real attributes.

3. The projected identity: the projected identity refers to the identity that is developed through engaging with the character, through the interaction of the first two identities.

However, Gee's conception of the virtual self here is located in gaming and the character within the games, and his notion of identity here seems to equate with 'role' rather than identity per se. Further, he has argued that identities are projected identities, but this introduces interesting psychoanalytic difficulties. Projections are usually unwanted feelings that we invariably choose not to own. We therefore believe that someone else is thinking/feeling them instead, such as anger or judgement (see, e.g. Jung, 1977). Avatars in VWs seem, in general, to capture wanted elements, or the chosen components of our identities that we wish to present to/in the world. Thus, in VWs, it would seem that the identities presented are more likely to be the functional or ideal sides rather than the projected 'unwanted' sides.

Further confusions arise through choices of representation, for example, whether to ensure the avatar looks 'more like us,' since this may create a great sense of comfort and decrease disease or not, since it forces us to confront how we see ourselves and how we want others to see us. However, the location of one's avatar in VWs poses particular complexities, because of the interaction of five interrelated concerns that play out in the 'social space.' These are:

- The 'real' body, in the sense the interlocutor of the avatar, the 'author.'
- The choice of physical representation and the way the avatar is presented to others.
- The relationship between the avatar and the author.
- The author's lived experience and the social representations made through the avatar.
- The intentional meanings represented through the avatar.

The assumption that follows is that there is a world out there (the real) that can be captured by a 'knowing' author through the careful transcription of one's roles into the avatar. Yet language and speech are not representations that mirror experience, but instead create it, thus the meanings ascribed and inscribed in and through avatars are always on the move.

In the past, Haraway (1991) and Hayles (1999) were at the forefront of discussions about identity in digital spaces, and Ito et al. (2010) have been influential in the work that has examined how youth culture and identity might be understood. Since then, a raft of sociologists have examined identity, and there is now a broad literature on identity. The result then is that computers change not only what we do, but also how we think about the world and ourselves. Further, Jandrić (2020) makes an important distinction between the functional copying of human minds, on the one hand, and the problem of the continuity of human consciousness, on the other, which would be broken if transferred to another substrate. This reminds us of the nature of embodiment in its literal sense of being within a body, and the idea of an embodied agent comes to mind, as opposed to other interfaces, for interacting with a digital immortal (e.g. via a computer interface). The idea of embodied cognition shapes the different aspects of cognition and therefore any kind of digital afterlife or digital immortal is unlikely to be an embodied robot of ourselves or others, unlike, for example, the character Rachel in Cass Hunter's (2018) *The After Wife*. Instead, it will be more closely aligned to VR, immersion and with the online experiences to which we have grown accustomed. Yet it is important to note that many of the debates in the area of AI tend to sidestep the issues of the relationships between human and machines. In a world where online learning, machines and people coalesce, there is often a sense that there is symmetry in the relationship between computers and people. Jones (2018) argued:

> Experience can be thought of as either the essential distinguishing component of the individual human subject, or experience can be understood as the subjective component of one kind of element in a wider assemblage of humans and machines. In the later understanding of experience in assemblages human experience does not separate the human actor from other actors in a network and they are understood symmetrically. (p. 39)

Indeed, during the COVID-19 pandemic people, were constantly tethered to machines and reliant on them for communication with loved ones, shopping and sustaining their mental health. Yet in the debate between Fuller and Latour about whether a distinction between humans and non-humans was required for research purposes, Latour argued that 'all phenomena should be treated equally, whether it comes from something human, natural or artificial' (Barron, 2003) but this clearly results in what Fuller calls the 'abdication of responsibility'(Fuller & Jandrić, 2019). It seems to be increasingly clear that there is an array of unanswered questions about whether there can be any kind of real symmetry between people and machines and perhaps more importantly how the many ethical concerns should be managed, evident in debates about face recognition and face verification.

Claims and Concerns

There are wide concerns that much is being made of the metaverse and that the propaganda has for a period been led by Mark Zuckerberg's desire to promote his empire, built from his creation of Facebook in 2004. For example, Freuler and Cruz (2021) suggest he is redirecting attention away from a public scrutiny as a public relations strategy in the face of downward trends in his business. What is also interesting amidst the publicity are the claims being made:

> Claim 1: the metaverse is here and available, and it is a multiuser environment that merges physical reality and the digital (Schlemmer & Backes, 2015).
>
> Claim 2: the metaverse can already enable seamless embodied communication between platforms, games, AR and VR in real time (Hwang & Chien, 2022).
>
> Claim 3: the metaverse will be available and accessible for everyone, everywhere and it will be a single metaverse, not several metaverses or multiverses (Parisi, 2021).
>
> Claim 4: education in the metaverse will necessarily enable rich, hybrid, formal and informal active learning where students are co-owners of the virtual spaces (Mystakidis, 2022).

Concerns

There are suggestions that education should remain unchanged and material spaces should be controlled and managed by lecturers, as exemplified by the arguments of Biesta (2019). This therefore implies that the metaverse can just be melded on to current education practices such as the transmission of knowledge and the use of physical classrooms being the primary means of learning. It is also argued that learning in the metaverse will enable rich hybrid forms of online learning and that 'avatar body language and facial expression fidelity will enable virtual participation to be equally effective' (Mystakidis, 2022, p. 494). Yet there are also concerns about the way in which the metaverse will extend data harvesting, which Origgi and Ciranna (2017) suggest may result in epistemic harm 'by depriving people of their credibility about themselves.' They suggest that data mining, tracking and the lack of control over our online identities result in new forms of injustice, which then make us less credible as witnesses of our own lives.

At the same time, it seems the metaverse will increasingly become a space of control and surveillance, shaping labour and the labour market. Zuboff (2019) argues that we have already entered a new and unprecedented era, that of surveillance capitalism, in which the dominance of the main technology companies, notably Google, Facebook, Apple and Amazon, have adapted capitalism to suit their own ends and over which the rest of us appear to have little or no control. The metaverse will be surveillance capitalism writ large with people being organized and guided by the corporate machine. However, to counter this it will be vital to

> …focus our attention on the power of big tech which directly threatens our emancipatory capabilities… We need to make sure that the spaces of the future enable change, agency, co-production, negotiation, cooperation and resistance.
>
> **(Freuler and Cruz, 2021)**

Conclusion

Education in and through the metaverse requires that we use new digital spaces for cooperation, co-production and change rather than control and surveillance. In practice, this means that a range of learning approaches need to be adopted across all sectors of education. Teaching should not be about the transmission of a body of knowledge, but instead about supporting learners to become critical beings who are aware of fake news, control and surveillance. Chapter 2 suggests a range of learning approaches that are central to effective learning and education in the metaverse.

References

Azuma, R. T. (1997). A survey of augmented reality. *Presence: Teleoperators & Virtual Environments*, *6*(4), 355–385.

Barron, C. (2003). A strong distinction between humans and non-humans is no longer required for research purposes: A debate between Bruno Latour and Steve Fuller. *History of the Human Sciences*, *16*(2), 77–99. https://doi.org/10.1177/09526951030160020004

Biesta, G. (2019). Teaching for the possibility of being taught: World-centred education in an age of learning. *E-Journal of Philosophy of Education*, *4*, 55–69.

Bishop, G., & Fuchs, H. (1992). Research directions in virtual environments: Report of an NSF invitational workshop, March 23-24, 1992, University of North Carolina at Chapel Hill. *SIGGRAPH Computer Graphics*, *26*(3), 153–177. https://doi.org/10.1145/142413.142416

Bogan, M., Bybee, S., & Bahlis, J. (2019). Increasing XR Technology's Return on Investment through Media Analysis. In Interservice/Industry Training, Simulation, and Education Conference (I/ITSEC), Orlando, Florida, USA. Retrieved from http://www.bnhexpertsoft.com/wpcontent/uploads/2020/03/ITSEC_2019_Paper_CAE_BNH.pdf.

Burden, D., & Savin-Baden, M. (2019). *Virtual humans: Today and tomorrow*. CRC Press.

Burden, D., & Savin-Baden, M. (2024). *The metaverse: A critical introduction*. CRC Press.

Burden, B., Savin-Baden, M., & Mason Robbie, V. (2022). Development of a pedagogy 'Biscuit Book' for the design of Virtual Reality experiences: A literature review. Daden Ltd.

Chayka, K. (2021, August 5). Facebook wants us to live in the metaverse. What does that even mean? *The New Yorker*. https://www.newyorker.com/culture/infinite-scroll/facebook-wants-us-to-live-in-the-metaverse

de la Peña, N., Weil, P., Llobera, J., Giannopoulos, E., Pomés, A., Spanlang, B., Friedman, D., Sanchez-Vives, M. V., & Slater, M. (2010). Immersive journalism: Immersive virtual reality for the first-person experience of news. *Presence: Teleoperators and Virtual Environments, 19*(4), 291–301. https://doi.org/10.1162/PRES_a_00005

Freuler, J. O., & Cruz, M. F. S. (2021, December 8). Zuckerberg's metaverse is a natural extension of capitalist extraction of our data. *openDemocracy*. https://www.opendemocracy.net/en/oureconomy/zuckerbergs-metaverse-is-a-natural-extension-of-capitalist-extraction-of-our-data/

Fuller, S., & Jandrić, P. (2019). The postdigital human: Making the history of the future. *Postdigital Science and Education, 1*(1), 190–217.

Gee, J. P. (2004). *What video games have to teach us about learning and literacy*. Palgrave Macmillan.

Haraway, D. (Ed.). (1991). A cyborg manifesto: Science, technology, and socialist-feminism in the late twentieth century. In *Simians, cyborgs and women: The reinvention of nature* (pp. 149–181). Routledge.

Hayles, K. (1999). *How we became posthuman: Virtual bodies in cybernetics, literature and informatics*. University of Chicago Press.

Hunter, C. (2018). *The After Wife: A moving and emotional story about a family keeping a big secret*. Trapeze.

Hwang, G. J., & Chien, S. Y. (2022). Definition, roles, and potential research issues of the metaverse in education: An artificial intelligence perspective. *Computers and Education: Artificial Intelligence, 3*. https://doi.org/10.1016/j.caeai.2022.100082

Ito, M., Baumer, S., Bittanti, M., Boyd, D., Cody, R., Herr-Stephenson, B., Horst, H. A., Lange, P. G., Mahendran, D., & Martínez, K. Z. (2010). *Hanging out, messing around, and geeking out*. MIT Press Cambridge, MA.

Jandrić, P. (2020). Postdigital afterlife: A philosophical framework. In M. Savin-Baden, & V. Mason-Robbie (Eds.), *Digital afterlife* (pp. 173–188). CRC Press.

Jones, C. (2018). Experience and networked learning: Reflections and challenges. In N. Bonderup Dohn, S. Cramer, J. A. Some, M. de Laat, & T. Ryberg (Eds.), *Networked learning: Reflections and challenges* (pp. 39–55). Springer International.

Jung, C. G. (1977). *The symbolic life: Miscellaneous writings the collected works of C. G. Jung*, (Vol. 18). Princeton University Press.

Knox, J. (2022). The metaverse, or the serious business of tech frontiers. In *Postdigital science and education* (Vol. 4, Issue 2, pp. 207–215). Springer International Publishing. https://doi.org/10.1007/s42438-022-00300-9

Lee, L.-H., Braud, T., Zhou, P., Wang, L., Xu, D., Lin, Z., Kumar, A., Bermejo, C., & Hui, P. (2021). *All one needs to know about metaverse: A complete survey on technological singularity, virtual ecosystem, and research agenda*. http://arxiv.org/abs/2110.05352

Lewis, C. S. (1952). *Mere Christianity*. Fount Paperbacks.

Luck, M., & Clarke, S. (2022). Transformative technologies, the status quo, and (Religious) Institutions. In M. Boylan & W. Teays (Eds.), *Ethics in the AI, technology, and information age* (pp. 35–48). Rowman & Littlefield Publishers.

Mårell-Olsson, E. (2019). University students as co-creators in designing gamification teaching activities using emergent technologies in Swedish K-12 education. *IxD&A: Interaction Design and Architecture(s), 42*, 47–69.

Mystakidis, S. (2022). Metaverse. *Encyclopedia, 2*(1), 486–497. https://doi.org/10.3390/encyclopedia2010031

Ning, H., Wang, H., Lin, Y., Wang, W., Dhelim, S., Farha, F., Ding, J., & Daneshmand, M. (2021). A survey on metaverse: The state-of-the-art, technologies, applications, and challenges. *IEEE Internet of Things Journal, 10*(16), 14671–14688. https://doi.org/10.1109/JIOT.2023.3278329

Origgi, G., & Ciranna, S. (2017). Epistemic injustice: The case of digital environments. In I. J. Kidd, J. Medina, & G. Pohlhaus (Eds.), *The Routledge handbook of epistemic injustice* (pp. 1–9; 303–312). Routledge.

Parisi, P. (2021, August 22). *The seven rules of the metaverse*. https://medium.com/meta-verses/the-seven-rules-of-the-metaverse-7d4e06fa864c

Ruthberg, J. S., Tingle, G., Tan, L., Ulrey, L., Simonson-Shick, S., Enterline, R., Eastman, H., Mlakar, J., Gotschall, R., Henninger, E., Griswold, M. A., & Wish-Baratz, S. (2020). Mixed reality as a time-efficient alternative to cadaveric dissection. *Medical Teacher, 42*, 896–901.

Sacks, R., Perlman, A., & Barak, R. (2013). Construction safety training using immersive virtual reality. *Construction Management and Economics, 31*(9), 1005–1017.

Savin-Baden, M. (2023). *Digital and postdigital learning for changing universities*. Routledge.

Schlemmer, E., & Backes, L. (2015). *Learning in metaverses*. IGI Global. https://doi.org/10.4018/978-1-4666-6351-0

Stenhouse, L. (1975). *An introduction to curriculum research and development*. Heinemann.

Tlili, A., Huang, R., Shehata, B., Liu, D., Zhao, J., Metwally, A. H. S., Wang, H., Denden, M., Bozkurt, A., Lee, L. H., Beyoglu, D., Altinay, F., Sharma, R. C., Altinay, Z., Li, Z., Liu, J., Ahmad, F., Hu, Y., Salha, S., … Burgos, D. (2022). Is Metaverse in education a blessing or a curse: A combined content and bibliometric analysis. In *Smart learning environments* (Vol. 9, Issue 1). Springer. https://doi.org/10.1186/s40561-022-00205-x

Zuboff, S. (2019). *The age of surveillance capitalism: The fight for a human future at the new frontier of power*. Profile Books.

2

Approaches to Learning

Introduction

This chapter provides a detailed examination of the different approaches to learning that are relevant to the metaverse. It begins by discussing learning theories and explores how these may or may not enable effective learning for students. The second section of the chapter examines different types of teaching, from traditional lecture-based learning to more learner-centred approaches such as problem-based learning (PBL) and collaborative learning. The final section of the chapter suggests particular modes of learning that may easily be adapted for the metaverse.

Learning Theories

There are broadly five approaches to learning theory, namely:

- Behavioural
- Cognitive
- Humanistic
- Developmental
- Critical awareness

Behavioural Theories

Early behavioural theories took too simplistic view of learning and have resulted in some lasting influences, such as the development of the use of performance objectives in learning. These behavioural objectives are usually manifested in programmed instruction, competency-based education and skill development and training that are not suitable for understanding the complex learning that we seek in academe, such as learning multifaceted

DOI: 10.1201/9781003413875-3

ideas and theories and developing metacognitive skills. For behaviourists, learning activities should be organized to optimize the acquisition of information and routine skill, which is too confining for learning in the metaverse.

Early models, such as that of Thorndike (1913), provided an understanding of improvement of learning through feedback, clear goals and practice, concepts that underpin many forms of PBL. In addition, Hull's work and his notion of Drive Reduction Theory (Hull, 1943) promotes a key aspect of learning, which asserts that students should be motivated as stakeholders in attempting to solve problems and thereby learn effectively. One of the issues with behavioural notions is that they generally assert that we cannot evaluate learning except through behavioural changes. Thus, they see learning as a relatively permanent change in behaviour brought about as a result of experience or practice. This makes the product or outcome the most important factor, rather than the iterative process itself. There are other strange assumptions that emerge from the behavioural tradition as well, such as the belief that outcomes and benchmarking standards will somehow make learning better or will prove competence to practice or even make what is taught auditable across the same subject in different universities.

The use of behavioural approaches in the metaverse can result in highly structured over-managed learning which in general does not fit easily with fluid and creative spaces.

Cognitive Theories

The promoters of the cognitive tradition (Ausubel et al., 1978) have argued that new information has to be interpreted in terms of both prior knowledge and shared perspectives. Thus, the existing cognitive structure is the principal factor influencing meaningful learning. In practice, this means that meaningful material can only be learned in relation to a previously learned background of relevant concepts. The notion of approaches to learning is rooted in the cognitive tradition, emerging from the work of Marton and Säljö (1976) who distinguished two different approaches to learning: those learners who could concentrate on memorizing (surface approaches to learning) and those who put meaning in their own terms (deep approaches to learning). Entwistle (1981) at the University of Lancaster, United Kingdom, extended the work of Marton and Säljö in what is known as the Lancaster studies, which were first undertaken to identify the factors associated with students' academic success and failure at university. Entwistle then built upon the work on surface and deep approaches to learning as well as the work of Pask (1988), who claimed that there are two general categories of learning strategy which can be identified in cognitive tasks: holists, students who identify the main parameters of a system and then filled in the details; and serialist students, who progressively work through details to build up the complete picture as they progress. Ultimately Entwistle extended the definitions of deep and surface categories and also added a third category: a strategic approach. These three approaches are thus delineated by the following characteristics:

- *Deep approach:*
  - Intention to understand.
  - Vigorous interaction with content.
  - Relate new ideas to previous knowledge.
  - Relate concepts to everyday experience.
  - Relate evidence to conclusions.
  - Examine the logic of the argument.
- *Surface approach:*
  - Intention to complete task requirements.
  - Memorize information needed for assessments.
  - Failure to distinguish principles from examples.
  - Treat task as an external imposition.
  - Focus on discrete elements without integration.
  - Unreflectiveness about purpose or strategies.
- *Strategic approach:*
  - Intention to obtain the highest possible grades.
  - Organize time and distribute effort to the greatest effect.
  - Ensure conditions and materials for studying appropriately.
  - Use previous exam papers to predict questions.
  - Be alert to cues about the marking scheme.

One of the central issues to emerge from this tradition was that of the 'learning context.' The notion of learning context is important because although students' learning strategies and the processes they have adopted do have a certain stability over time, the learning context affects the quality of student learning (Entwistle et al., 1984). The acknowledgment of the importance of the learning context has thus begun to raise concerns not only about student learning *per se* but also has brought to the fore the importance of the learner as a person whose experience is often somewhat marginalized in studies about ways in which students learn.

By recognizing both students' approaches to learning and the importance of learning context will ensure that learning activities designed for the metaverse will promote effective student learning.

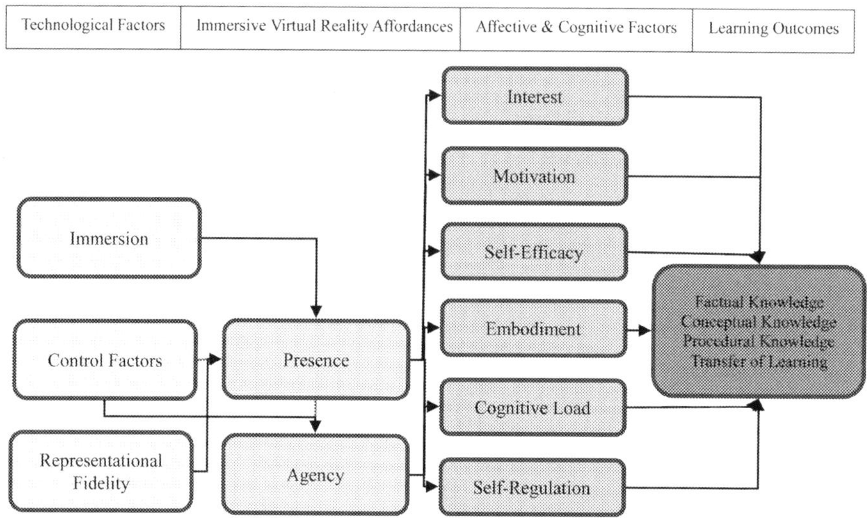

FIGURE 2.1 Overview of CAMIL (From Makransky & Petersen, 2021).

Such activities might be linked to the work of Makransky and Petersen (2021) who suggests the Cognitive Affective Model of Immersive Learning (CAMIL) as a useful model for learning in virtual reality. The model is shown in Figure 2.1 and suggests that presence and agency are the central focus for learning and that immersion and control factors are influential in ensuring effective learning.

Humanistic Theories

Those in the humanistic field (Rogers, 1983) contend that significant learning is to be obtained only within situations that are both defined by and under the control of the learner. Here the aims of education are upon self-development and the development of a fully functioning person. The prior experience of the learner is acknowledged, and it is also recognized that students may be constrained by their own negative experiences of learning. The teacher (termed in this tradition facilitator) helps to provide a supportive environment in which learners are enabled to recognize and explore their needs. Humanist theorists believe learners have both affective and cognitive needs, so the goal of learning is to become self-actualized and autonomous, and education should facilitate the development of the whole person. Those in the humanistic field contend that significant learning is to be obtained only within situations that are both defined by and under the control of the learner (e.g. Rogers, 1983). Learning in this tradition is thus seen as involving the whole person, and not just the intellect, thus educators in this tradition aim to liberate learners and allow them freedom to learn.

The challenge in the metaverse is that if learning activities are too loosely defined, learners become lost in learning. Whilst disjunction (becoming stuck in learning) can be a useful growth point (Savin-Baden, 2006), it can also feel disabling for students; and so tutors need to provide a degree of guidance when adopting a humanistic approach. An example of this in the metaverse would be to ask students to design a learning game for young children but provide a few guidelines or parameters. Whilst this approach might inspire some students, others would feel unsure and stuck.

Developmental Theories

The developmental theorists offer us models that in many ways seem to take account of cognition and development. The teacher's concern here is in enabling students to develop both understandings of the nature of knowledge and ways of handling different conceptions of the world, so that knowledge acquisition is seen as an active process. It has been from this field that a number of innovative studies have arisen. For example, from a qualitative study of men at Harvard, Perry (1970) devised nine positions that described how students' conceptions of the nature and origins of knowledge evolved. This classic study put issues of learner experience centre stage and argued that students proceed through a sequence of developmental stages. In this description of the attainment of intellectual and emotional maturity, the student moves from an authoritarian, polarized view of the world, through stages of uncertainty and accepting uncertainty, to finally an understanding of the implications of managing this uncertainty. The student then accepts the need for orientation through a commitment to values and eventually gains a distinct identity through a thoughtful and constantly developing commitment to a set of values. Belenky et al. (1986) were stimulated by Perry's work to explore diverse women's perspectives, and they identified five categories of 'ways of knowing' and from this drew conclusions about the way women see truth, knowledge and authority. For example, women began from a position of silence where they saw themselves as mindless, voiceless and subject to the whims of external authority. In later stages, women constructed knowledge; this was where the women viewed all knowledge as related to the context in which it occurred and experienced themselves as creators of knowledge. It is the work of these developmental theorists that seems to offer some of the more tenable models of learning. They are models which, to a degree, acknowledge that what is missing from many curricula is a recognition of the role and relevance of learning from and through experience, which can prompt the shaping and reconstructing of people's lives as learners.

The challenge of using this approach is gauging which activities may provoke development for students in the metaverse. A useful model to help with this is Activity Theory-based Model of Serious Games conceptual framework which requires tutors to map the pedagogical elements and learning outcomes with game elements whilst at the same time maintaining the balance between entertainment and learning (Callaghan et al., 2018).

Critical Awareness Theories

Critical awareness theories are seen as not simply another perspective on adult learning but rather a shift in ideology. The ideals of this tradition stem largely from theorists such as Freire (1972, 1974) who argued that social and historical forces shape the processes through which people come to know themselves and develop their view of the world. Learning is therefore seen to occur in a social and cultural context, and this necessarily influences what and how people learn. Learners therefore must seek to transcend the constraints their world places upon them in order to liberate themselves and become critically aware. Another contributor to these theories is Mezirow (1981) with his notions of perspective transformation and transformative learning. These theories share common assumptions: people having control over their own situations, the capability to reflect upon them and take action to change them; people constructing their own reality to serve different purposes which they validate through interaction and communication with others; and the transformation of individuals resulting in social transformation. Learning is therefore seen to occur in a social and cultural context, and this necessarily influences what and how people learn. Learners therefore must seek to transcend the constraints their world places upon them in order to liberate themselves and become critically aware. More recently, the work of hooks (1994) has helped to further this work, and to some extent Pratt (Pratt & Smulders, 2016), but it remains a tradition that has gained relatively little attention, although it may soon do so with the onset of the Web 4.0 movement, the increasing shift towards learning as social networking and the interest in Bauman's (2000, 2013) work on liquidity.

In terms of the metaverse to date, there is little discussion about the critical awareness tradition. However, there is related work in this area, such as the notion of Radical digital citizenship and fake news. Emejulu and McGregor (2019) used the term Radical digital citizenship as a result of their analysis of the impact of technology on our lives socially, politically, economically and environmentally. It requires that people take a stance and take action to create and build new technological and emancipatory practices. In practice, this means recognizing digital inequalities and problematizing dominant models and ideas about technology. Fake news is a term that was popularized during the 2016 US elections in order to describe both inaccurate news and staged news shows. Otrel-Cass and Fasching (2021) explored young people's encounters with fake news and found that, in order to enable them to understand the potential instances of dupery, teaching in this area needed to be personalized to reflect students' experiences of online and fake news.

TABLE 2.1 Learning Theories

The Theory	Key Concepts	Challenges for Learning in the Metaverse
Behavioural	• We need specific goals and clear objectives if we are to learn. • The learning experience should be task-orientated.	1. The focus is on incentives – which do not motivate everyone. 2. The assumption is that having passed the test you can do the job.
Cognitive	• We each have our own cognitive structure which must be accommodated. • We can only learn new information in relation to what we already know.	1. Overemphasis on learning styles at the expense of content. 2. Tendency to categorize people into 'types' of learners.
Humanistic	• The learning needs to be controlled by us as the learners, not the tutor. • Emphasis must be on our freedom to choose the approach.	1. Too much freedom can be disabling. 2. People are not always sure what they want or need to learn.
Developmental	• Learning needs to be part of our progressive development. • We need to see knowledge acquisition as relevant to where we are and what we want.	1. Overemphasis on experiential approaches to learning at the expense of efficiency. 2. Tendency to spend time reflecting on mistakes rather than looking forward.
Critical awareness	• We all have our values, including tutors. Learning is not value-free. • Learning always takes place in a social and cultural context.	1. Difficult to manage power relations between teacher and learner to ensure 'real' equality. 2. Can be seen as overly politicized.

One straightforward way to understand the differences in these learning theories is to consider how they have an impact on learning in the metaverse, which are summarized in Table 2.1.

Types of Learning

In former years, the university concentrated on lectures and seminars. However, following the work of authors such as Dewey (1938), Rogers (1983) and Entwistle et al. (1984), there has been an increasing realization that learning which focusses on knowledge acquisition has resulted in surface approaches to learning. It became apparent that there was a need to recognize that students have different approaches to learning and that university teaching needed to reflect this. Whilst there have been arguments that students can be categorized into particular learning styles, these have largely been discarded in favour of recognizing that all learners are different and each have a distinct learner identity.

The concept of learning styles has suggested that an individual has a consistent approach to organizing information and processing it in the learning environment, yet the model of learning styles developed by Kolb and Fry (1975), in which they suggest there are four learning styles: converger, diverger, assimilator and accommodator, is rather too tidy. They argue that a complete learner is someone who has managed to integrate bipolar components of the four learning styles. Although this is a useful model for helping learners to understand something of their approach to learning, it is problematic in that different learning environments demand different learning styles and thus the complete learner must be someone who can either adapt their style or someone who applies a consistent learning strategy across all environments.

Learner identity expresses the idea that the interaction of learner and learning, in whatever framework, formulates a particular kind of identity. The notion of learner identity encompasses positions which students take up in learning situations, whether consciously or unconsciously. Invariably, school-leavers attending university have an identity largely formulated through their schooling and arrive at university with a sense of whether they are deemed to be successes or failures by peers and external authorities. These students understand themselves in terms of how they are seen as learners by others. They realize components of their learner identity through the eyes of others, even if they cannot define it for themselves. For more experienced students, learner identity is not related to how they are seen by others but instead through the conditions under which they perceive themselves to be learning. Thus, learner identity incorporates not only a sense of how one has come to be a learner in a given context but also the perceptions about when and how one actually learns. As a result, learner identity also encompasses affective components of learning that often seem of little matter to those in the business of creating learning environments in institutional settings. Issues of trust and fear that emerge through critical reflection such as questioning, reframing assumptions, learning together, sharing and evaluating researched information, undertaking presentations and arguing one's point are rarely acknowledged in learning environments (Brookfield, 1995). Still, learner identity is not to be seen as a stable entity but as something people use to make sense of themselves, and the ways in which they learn best in relation to other people and the learning environments in which they are learning.

Bernstein (2000) argues that through experiences as students, individuals within higher education are in the process of identity formation. He suggests that this process may be seen as the construction of pedagogic identities that will change according to the different relationships that occur between society, higher education and knowledge. Thus, pedagogic identities are characterized by the emphases of the time. For example, in the traditional disciplines of the 1960s, students were inducted into the particular pedagogical customs of those disciplines, whereas pedagogic identities of the 1990s were characterized by a common set of market-related, transferable skills. The difference between learner identity and pedagogic identity is that, whilst pedagogic identities are seen to be those that arise out of contemporary culture and technological change, learner identities emerge from the process through which students seek to transcend subjects and disciplines, and the structures embedded in higher education. Thus, in developing their learner identities, some students are enabled to shift beyond frameworks which are imposed by culture, validated through political agenda or supplied by academics. They are facilitated in developing for themselves, possibly through learning such as PBL, the formulation of a learner identity that emerges from challenging the frameworks, rather than having the frameworks and systems imposed upon them.

The notion of the learning context has been discussed in a variety of ways by authors who have predominantly been concerned with students' learning experiences. For example, Ramsden (1992) suggested that a student's perception of the learning context is an integral component of his learning. The learning context is created through students' experiences of the constituents of the programmes on which they are studying, namely, teaching methods, assessment mechanisms and the overall design of the curriculum. Students, Ramsden suggests, respond to the situation they perceive, which may differ from that which has been defined by educators. Yet, however much it is denied, educators tend to think of learning contexts as static environments. Each year the programme or module is on offer and is usually fairly similar to the one offered the previous year and so students are taught in the same way with the same material. It is as if people, and students in particular, are put into contexts and watched whilst they move about inside them. Yet learning contexts are transient in nature, and much of the real learning that takes place for students occurs beyond the parameters of the presented material. Taylor (1986) has argued that since educational programmes are temporary environments, it is important to raise students' awareness of the changing natures of the learning environment, peers, tutors and themselves. Therefore, recognition of students' perceptions of the formal learning context is key to facilitating students' ability to manage learning effectively. However, we argue that the concept of learning context incorporates more than just the students' experiences of the component's teaching methods, assessment mechanisms and the overall design of the curriculum. Equally, learning context comprises more than that which can be defined according to the situation and perhaps even the disciplinary area of study. Thus, the notion of learning context incorporates the interplay of all the values, beliefs, relationships, frameworks and external structures that operate within a given learning environment. Learning context also incorporates the way in which the curriculum is situated within the university and the broader framework of higher education, and thus the way it is situated within such systems and frameworks will affect what it means to be a learner in such a context. Furthermore, the notion of learning context does not only comprise the formal curriculum but also the informal ones – the ones students create for themselves. This might suggest that the smallest component of any learning context could be said to be the formal curriculum, since the learning context is in reality rarely bounded by formal structures but instead by those who comprise and define it.

Linking Teaching Modes with the Metaverse

The following section suggests that some modes of learning are more adaptable to the metaverse then others. In practice, modes that promote collaboration, interaction, application, engagement and deep approaches to learning are ones that are effective in the metaverse. This means that students enjoy and value learning, and are able to retain and use what they have learned more successfully than teacher-led and lecture-based approaches to learning.

Lecture-based Learning

This form of learning has been one of the most used and traditional forms of learning in universities and business settings. Here students are provided with a body of knowledge in the form of content provided through notes or a PowerPoint by a tutor with a view that by passing on this knowledge students will learn and understand it. Generally, there is no interaction although there may be opportunities for questions at the end. The tutor is in charge of the knowledge presented, and students learn through note-taking and, in general, adopt a surface approach to learning. Lectures can be used in the metaverse in spaces such as virtual worlds (VWs), but these tend to be no more effective than lectures undertaken face-to-face. Examples of lectures in the metaverse can be seen in VWs such as *Second Life* (SL) where live lectures are streamed into a virtual space.

Problem-solving Learning

This is the type of teaching many staff have been using for years, and the focus is upon giving students a lecture or an article to read and then a set of questions based upon the information given. Students are expected to find the solutions to these questions and bring them to a seminar as a focus for discussion. Problem scenarios here are set within and bounded by a discrete subject or disciplinary area. In some curricula, students are given specific training in problem-solving techniques, but in many cases, they are not. The focus in this kind of learning is largely upon acquiring the answers expected by the lecturer, answers that are rooted in the information supplied in some way to the students. Thus, the solutions are always linked to a specific curricula content which is seen as vital for students to cover in order for them to be competent and effective practitioners. The solutions are therefore bounded by the content, and students are expected to explore little extra material other than that provided, in order to discover the solutions. These bounded problems are often used for small group learning activities when students are learning using different media within and across the metaverse. In practice, students might be presented with a group problem to solve and expected to work together on a Writeboard, VW and virtual platform; they might be expected to create a blog to share their work and present their solution in a Microsoft Teams event with the rest of the student cohort.

Problem-based Learning

Problem-based learning is different from problem-solving learning. In PBL, the focus is on organizing the curricular content around problem scenarios rather than subjects or disciplines. Students work in groups or teams to solve or manage these situations, but they are not expected to acquire a predetermined series of 'right answers.' Instead, they are expected to engage with the complex situation presented to them and decide what information they need to learn and what skills they need to gain in order to manage the situation effectively. There are many different ways of implementing PBL, but the underlying philosophies associated with it as an approach are broadly more student-centred than those underpinning problem-solving learning. This is because students are offered opportunities, through PBL, to explore a wide range of information, link the learning with their own needs as learners and develop independence in inquiry. Problem-based learning is thus an approach to learning that is characterized by flexibility and diversity in the sense that it can be implemented in a variety of ways in and across different subjects and disciplines in diverse contexts. As such it can therefore look very different to different people at different moments in time, depending on the staff and students involved in the programmes utilizing it. However, what will be similar will be the focus of learning around problem scenarios rather than discrete subjects or disciplines. Problem-based learning has been used extensively in the metaverse as it is such a flexible approach. Whilst this is discussed in detail in Chapter 3, it is useful to note that most research, to date, has examined students' experiences in VWs (Savin-Baden, 2013) and live chat in VWs (Steils et al., 2015). Practicing skills within a VW offers advantages over learning through real-life practice, in particular, the exposure of learners to a wide range of scenarios (more than they are likely to meet in a standard face-to-face programme) at a time and pace convenient to the learner. Consistent feedback as exemplified in the Problem-based Learning in Virtual Interactive Educational Worlds (PREVIEW) demonstrator project that investigated the creation and testing of PBL scenarios in SL (Beaumont et al., 2014; Conradi et al., 2009) can also be provided easily.

Experiential Learning

Dewey (1938) emphasized the human capacity to reconstruct experience and thus make meaning of it. Dewey believed in education as a process of continuous reconstruction and growth of experience. He believed that the role of the teacher was to organize learning activities which built on the previous experiences of the students and directed them to new experiences that furthered their growth, and that the curriculum should be closely tied to the students' experiences, developmentally appropriate and structured in ways that fostered continuity. Dewey opposed theories of knowledge that considered knowledge specialized and independent of its role in problem-solving inquiry. Whilst experiential learning is a broad approach the main focus here is that students encounter learning that is meaningful to them. Experiential learning can include problem-solving learning and PBL as well as work-based learning, reflection and encounter groups. In the metaverse practical and applied learning activities that link to students' future professions or world of work are generally seen as forms of experiential learning, such as teaching nurse prescribing within a VW (Dodds, 2021).

Collaborative Learning

Collaborative learning is an educational approach to teaching and learning that involves groups of learners working together to solve a problem, complete a task or create a product. Students are accountable to one another and work as a collective. In some forms of collaborative learning, students are assessed as a team. Proponents of this approach suggest that learning collaboration fosters in students a critical approach towards knowledge and enables them to develop a deep approach to learning (Laal & Ghodsi, 2012). Collaborative learning in the metaverse focusses not only on learning knowledge but also on developing team skills. The emphasis is on effective group work, tasks that promote debate and discussion, and team problem-solving. An example of this is game-based learning where teams have to work together to win a game as a collective such as *Circuit Warz*. The game is a team-based exercise where groups of students work together collaboratively and compete competitively against other teams to complete a virtual assault course, which in practice is a series of electronic and electrical circuits (puzzles) which need to be solved in order to complete the game and progress to the next level (Callaghan et al., 2012).

Conclusion

Theories of learning affect the way in which teaching and learning are implemented in the metaverse. Definitive behavioural approaches result in less creativity and more structured learning than other approaches. In contrast, humanistic approaches can result in students feeling lost with little structure and no direction. What is important in designing learning for the metaverse is understanding the purpose and context of learning, as well as how students learn and how their learner identity affects the way in which they learn. The application of these theories to the forms of learning for the metaverse is discussed in Chapter 3.

References

Ausubel, D. P., Novak, J. D., & Hanesian, H. (1978). *Educational psychology: A cognitive view*. Holt, Rinehart and Winston.

Bauman, Z. (2000). Living in the era of liquid modernity. *Cambridge Journal of Anthropology, 22*(2), 1–19.

Bauman, Z. (2013). *Liquid modernity*. Polity Press.

Beaumont, C., Savin-Baden, M., Conradi, E., & Poulton, T. (2014). Evaluating a Second Life problem-based learning (PBL) demonstrator project: What can we learn? *Interactive Learning Environments, 22*(1). https://doi.org/10.1080/10494820.2011.641681

Belenky, M. F., Clinchy, B. M., Goldberger, N. R., & Tarule, J. M. (1986). *Women's ways of knowing: The development of self, voice, and mind* (Vol. 15). Basic Books.

Bernstein, B. (2000). *Pedagogy, symbolic control, and identity: Theory, research, critique* (Vol. 5). Rowman & Littlefield.

Brookfield, S. D. (1995). *Becoming a critically reflective teacher*. John Wiley & Sons.

Callaghan, M. J., McCusker, K., Losada, J. L., Harkin, J. G., & Wilson, S. (2012). *Circuit Warz, the games; collaborative and competitive game-based learning in virtual worlds*. 2012 9th International Conference on Remote Engineering and Virtual Instrumentation (REV), 1–4.

Callaghan, M., McShane, N., Eguíluz, A., & Savin-Baden, M. (2018). Extending the activity theory based model for serious games design in engineering to integrate analytics. *International Journal of Engineering Pedagogy, 8*(1), 109–126.

Conradi, E., Kavia, S., Burden, D., Rice, A., Woodham, L., Beaumont, C., Savin-Baden, M., & Poulton, T. (2009). Virtual patients in a virtual world: Training paramedic students for practice. *Medical Teacher, 31*(8). https://doi.org/10.1080/01421590903134160

Dewey, J. (1938). *Experience and education* (60th anniversary). Kappa Delta Pi.

Dodds, N. (2021). Nurse prescribing: A real community of practice in the virtual world. *BMJ Supportive & Palliative Care, 11*(Suppl 2), A70–A71.

Emejulu, A., & McGregor, C. (2019). Towards a radical digital citizenship in digital education. *Critical Studies in Education, 60*(1), 131–147. https://doi.org/10.1080/17508487.2016.1234494

Entwistle, N. (1981). *Styles of learning and teaching*. John Wiley & Sons.

Entwistle, N., Hounsell, D., & Marton, F. (1984). *The experience of learning*. Scottish Academic Press.

Freire, P. (1972). *Pedagogy of the oppressed*. Penguin Books.

Freire, P. (1974). Education: The practice of freedom. Writers and Readers Co-operative.

hooks, B. (1994). Teaching to transgress: Education as the practice of freedom. Routledge.

Hull, C. L. (1943). *Principles of behavior: An introduction to behavior theory*. Appleton-Century.

Kolb, D. A., & Fry, R. (1975). Toward an applied theory of experiential learning. In C. Cooper (Ed.), *Studies of group process* (pp. 33–57). Wiley.

Laal, M., & Ghodsi, S. M. (2012). Benefits of collaborative learning. *Procedia – Social and Behavioral Sciences, 31*, 486–490. https://doi.org/10.1016/j.sbspro.2011.12.091

Makransky, G., & Petersen, G. B. (2021). The Cognitive Affective Model of Immersive Learning (CAMIL): A theoretical research-based model of learning in immersive virtual reality. *Educational Psychology Review, 33*(3), 937–958. https://doi.org/10.1007/s10648-020-09586-2

Marton, F., & Säljö, R. (1976). On qualitative differences in learning: I—Outcome and process. *British Journal of Educational Psychology, 46*(1), 4–11.

Mezirow, J. (1981). A critical theory of adult learning and education. *Adult Education, 32*(1), 3–24.

Otrel-Cass, K., & Fasching, M. (2021). Postdigital truths: Educational reflections on fake news and digital identities. In M. Savin-Baden (Ed.), *Postdigital humans: Transitions, transformations and transcendence* (pp. 89–108). Springer International Publishing. https://doi.org/10.1007/978-3-030-65592-1_6

Pask, G. (1988). Learning strategies, teaching strategies, and conceptual or learning style. In R. R. Schmeck (Ed.), *Learning strategies and learning styles* (pp. 83–100). Springer US. https://doi.org/10.1007/978-1-4899-2118-5_4

Perry, W. G. (1970). *Forms of intellectual and ethical development in the college years: A scheme*. Holt, Rinehart, and Winston.

Pratt, D. D., & Smulders, D. (2016). *Five perspectives on teaching: Mapping a plurality of the good*. Krieger Publishing Company.

Ramsden, P. (1992). *Learning to teach in higher education*. Routledge.

Rogers, C. R. (1983). *Freedom to learn for the 80's* (Issue 371.39 R724f). Merrill Publishing.

Savin-Baden, M. (2006). Disjunction as a form of troublesome knowledge in problem-based learning. In J. H. F. Meyer & R. Land (Eds.), *Overcoming barriers to student understanding: Threshold concepts and troublesome knowledge*. Routledge. https://doi.org/10.4324/9780203966273

Savin-Baden, M. (2013). Spaces in between us: A qualitative study into the impact of spatial practice when learning in Second Life. *London Review of Education, 11*(1). https://doi.org/10.1080/14748460.2012.761820

Steils, N., Tombs, G., Mawer, M., Savin-Baden, M., & Wimpenny, K. (2015). Implementing the liquid curriculum: The impact of virtual world learning on higher education. *Technology, Pedagogy and Education, 24*(2). https://doi.org/10.1080/1475939X.2014.959454

Taylor, M. (1986). Learning for self-direction in the classroom: The pattern of a transition process. *Studies in Higher Education, 11*(1), 55–72.

Thorndike, E. L. (1913). *Educational psychology…* (Vol. 2). Teachers College, Columbia University.

3

Applied Models for Learning

Introduction

The main argument of this chapter is that whilst the concept of the metaverse is relatively new in university and college learning spaces, the metaverse and related technology have been in use since the late 1990s and came to prominence with the growth and use of virtual worlds (VWs) from 2003 onwards. This chapter begins by exploring the shifts from earlier versions to current versions of the metaverse. It then suggests different approaches to learning that might be used and explores learning in practice in the metaverse. The approaches vary from early versions, such as computer-supported collaborative learning and action learning, to more recent practices, such as games and gamification and the use of problem-based learning (PBL) in VWs.

From Early to Recent Understandings of Learning in the Metaverse

Since the advent and growth of teaching in virtual spaces there have been mounting arguments for the use of the metaverse for learning. In the early years, there was a degree of cynicism, with suggestion that learning in virtual spaces was not reflective of real life. Benford (2009) explored the relationship between real and virtual spaces, revisiting some previous work carried out, in order to examine the relationship between the structure of hybrid physical-digital spaces within the fields of ubiquitous computing, virtual reality (VR) and mixed reality. What is also important and interesting are the relationships between these spaces, in particular, the concepts of overlay and agency related to Milgram and Kishino's mixed reality continuum (Figure 3.1).

At one end of this continuum lies everyday physical reality and, at the other, is an immersed VR in which the participant is completely immersed in a computer-generated VW. The areas in between vary from spaces where

DOI: 10.1201/9781003413875-4

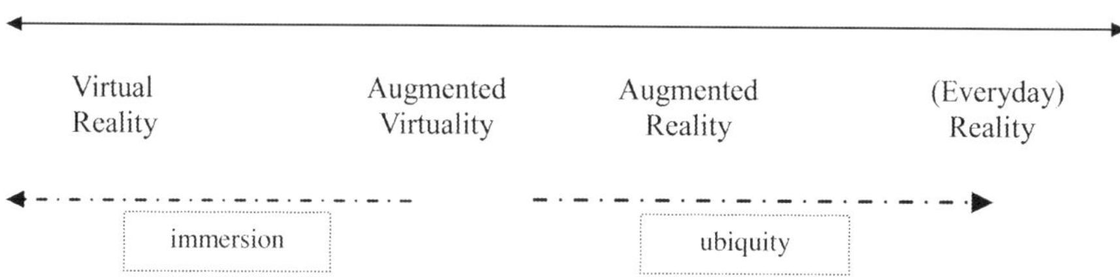

FIGURE 3.1 Mixed Reality Continuum (From Milgram & Kishino, 1994).

the participant primarily inhabits the physical but is working in the virtual, a managed learning environment could be located here, to augmented reality (AR) where the participant inhabits an online VW, but which is made live with information from the physical world; this could be the use of a VW with live feeds into learning scenarios, such as breaking news or weather reports. What we are seeing here is the relationship between adjacency and overlay. In VWs, feeds and real-life data are streamed in using overlay, so that this results in augmented virtuality. However, adjacency emerges from the concept of a mixed reality boundary, where there is a two-way portal between the physical and VWs. In practice, this means that in a physical office, it is possible to make it appear to be adjacent to a virtual office; it is as if the virtual office is an extension beyond the screen: they are not overlaid, they are next to each other. What is important for future developments of this work is that it offers a language and structure to begin to make sense not only of the developments occurring in the metaverse but also a means of examining the diversity of studies and activities taking place in other fields that can be used and built on for metaverse teaching in higher education.

More recently, Mikropoulos and Natsis (2011), in their review of studies of VR in the design of educational virtual environments (VEs), found that the theory or models to underpin the design or use of such environments were lacking. However, Dalgarno and Lee (2010) did present a model of learning in three-dimensional (3D) VEs. This model offers a comprehensive overview of how learning might work effectively, and we suggest it can be applied to learning in the metaverse. According to this model, a 3D VE is characterized by having the illusion of three dimensions, smooth temporal and physical changes, and a high level of interactivity, which provides a way of categorizing such an approach. Dalgarno and Lee identify representational fidelity and learner interaction as being the key characteristics of VR which lead to five affordances, so that 3D virtual learning environments can be used to:

- Facilitate learning tasks that lead to the development of enhanced spatial knowledge representation of the explored domain;
- Facilitate experiential learning tasks that would be impractical or impossible to undertake in the real world;

- Facilitate learning tasks that lead to increased intrinsic motivation and engagement;
- Facilitate learning tasks that lead to improved transfer of knowledge and skills to real situations through contextualization of learning and;
- Facilitate tasks that lead to richer and/or more effective collaborative learning than is possible with 2D alternatives.

Fowler (2015) argues that the Dalgarno and Lee model focusses on a technological viewpoint rather than on learning outcomes and proposes an extension of Dalgarno and Lee's model.

Learning design according to Fowler centres on designing learning that is student-centred so that the focus is on what it is the students are learning rather than what is being taught. More recent discussions have focussed on universal design for learning. Universal design argues for inclusivity both in terms of environments and also products. The idea is that it considers individual attributes in terms of disability, age, gender, race and ethnicity, native language and other diverse characteristics. The difficulty though with Fowler's model is the use of Bloom's taxonomy. The use of Bloom's (1956) taxonomy and the implementation of behavioural objectives used in relation to curricula needs to be challenged. Fowler's suggestion of using learning intentions with Bloom is misplaced as this results in both performativity and the large-scale discounting of disciplinary differences and discipline-based pedagogies – which seem to have endured despite the demands of behavioural curricular design. It would seem then, rather than adopting a notion of the curriculum whereby standardized designs are used for all disciplines, that instead curricula for the metaverse should be designed with criticality and troublesome knowledge as the centre point and not the counterpoint.

In a review of studies, learning taking place in VWs' (Loke, 2015) 11 theories were identified, of which seven were included and reviewed. This review analyzed theories used to guide research in VWs for education. The focus of the review was to examine which theories educators used to underpin educational VWs and to explore how applicable these were to VWs. The findings of this review were that, as with previous reviews, the predominant models used were experiential learning, situated learning, social constructivism, constructivism, self-efficacy theory, the projective identity model and presence theory. Loke argues that these provide an account of four learning mechanisms that explain how students learn in VWs:

- Reflection;
- Verbal interactions;
- Mental operations; and
- Vicarious experience.

However, the ability of users to learn embodied actions is questioned, and thus Loke (2015) calls for a new theory to explain how real-world skills can be learnt. This is important, because such learning is often cited as a primary reason for using VR.

Learning in Practice in the Metaverse

In the 2020s, virtual spaces have become a valued and valuable means of learning and have expanded into the notions of the metaverse. However, what is troublesome is that much of the research and literature to date focus on roadmaps for the metaverse (Lee et al., 2021), definitions of the metaverse (Ning et al., 2021) and reviews of the literature (Narin, 2021; Tlili et al., 2022). As yet there is relatively little research into learning in the metaverse or exploration of the impact of these technologies on students, but there are some. For example, Schott and Marshall (2021) discussed the role of virtual reality in fostering experiential education, in what they describe as the 'education landscape' from the user's perspective.

Perhaps one of the most valuable suggestions is that of Hwang and Chien (2022, p. 3) who present the following seven reasons for adopting the metaverse for educational purposes:

- To situate learners in a cognitive or skill-practising environment that could be risky or dangerous in the real world.
- To situate learners in certain contexts to experience and learn what they generally do not have the opportunity to do when involved in the real world.
- To enable learners to perceive or learn something that requires long-term involvement and practice.
- To encourage learners to try to create or explore something that they cannot afford to do in the real world owing to some practical reasons, such as the cost or the lack of real materials.
- To enable learners to have alternative thoughts and attempts regarding their careers or lives.
- To enable learners to perceive, experience or observe things from different perspectives or roles.
- To enable learners to learn to interact and even collaborate with people that they might not have opportunities to work with in the real world.
- To explore the potential or higher-order thinking of learners by engaging them in complex, diverse and authentic tasks.

It is important to underpin learning with theory because, whilst it is possible to base design on the assumptions of what might work, theory will guide design. In such approaches and frameworks, the subject matter or discipline is transcended, and it is the general principles that are important. These can provide guidance at the course level of design, whether VR is used exclusively or in a blended way and can also provide a way of thinking about the use of the metaverse. The following approaches were, in the main, developed in the 1990s but are still used, and have relevance here. The later approaches discussed in this section such as gaming and VWs gained most prominence in the 2000s.

Computer-Supported Collaborative Learning

The initial use of computer-supported collaborative learning was to encourage students to work as a collective. The focus was to help students to develop a shared understanding of the learning task, and this was influenced by the work of authors such as Resnick (1991). Early work by Roschelle and Teasley (1995) examined how two people developed a shared understanding of a task in a physics simulation. Their findings led them to assert that collaborative learning enabled the co-construction of shared understanding. More recent versions are based on the model by McConnell (2006) whereby students work in learning teams in order to define a problem relating to some form of professional or personal practice issue. The importance of this for the metaverse is in working collaboratively on a problem which can be shared with other teams. There is also a strong focus on understanding and critiquing the nature and complexity of teamwork, in order that team members are able to use this understanding to develop their own professional practice. Finally, students are expected to both self- and peer-assess and share their findings with one another. In this instantiation, there is a high emphasis on reflexivity and accountability to one another in terms of the development of one's own learning.

Action Learning

Action learning is based on the idea that through the process of reflection and action it is possible to solve problems. The idea is that a group of people come together to form an action learning set. The set work together over a stated period of time with the aim of 'getting things done' (McGill & Beaty, 2001, p. 1). In practice, this means that the set is formed, and each member brings a real-life problem they want help in solving. Action learning is a form of learning based on the interrelationship of learning and action, and thus the learning occurs through a continuous process of reflecting and acting by the individual on their problem. The essence of an action learning set is its focus on the individual and their future action (McGill & Beaty, 2001, pp. 14–15). Thus, in action learning, the members have more control over the group than many students would do in forms of learning that are team focussed, where the tutor may influence the learning agenda. Action learning sets are more individualized, freer flowing and centred upon personal learning and reflection in order to achieve effective action.

Problem-Orientated Learning

The arguments for problem-oriented learning (rather than PBL) have largely stemmed from Margetson's suggestions about the nature of knowledge, and in particular, his belief that some knowledge is not necessarily foundational to other knowledge. Margetson (1991) has suggested that the assumption that 'knowledge is certain' persists in higher education and that the assumed link between certainty and knowledge is used to justify didactic teaching. Margetson suggests that in order to move away from problems being 'based' on knowledge, we need to move away from the idea that knowledge is certain and thus use the term 'problem-oriented learning' as it allows for the use of open-ended problems; real problems, those to which solutions are not known. The focus on knowledge rather than collaboration means that problem-orientated learning is useful when learning through simulation and with virtual tutors where content coverage is important.

Work-based Learning

Work-based learning is used to describe learning through work so that learning occurs through engaging in a work role. The formulation of partnership is seen to have a central place in the discourses of work-based learning, and partnership as a concept operates in a variety of ways. For example, the funders of work-based learning are 'in partnership' with higher education institutions, or alternatively, an alliance takes the form of a partnership between the university and the learner. Work-based learning is an important development in many professions, but one of the key shifts it has prompted is a move away from higher education as front-end education that equips people for work. Instead, initiatives such as work-based learning have promoted ongoing learning, regular updating and continuing professional development, which in many ways have meant that higher education institutions have had to become more responsive to the needs of the learner. Work-based learning centres on learning through work and tends to be individually guided and focussed on solving problems in the immediate work environment. However, this form of learning is often linked with workplace simulation and the use of AR.

Project-based Learning

Project-based learning would be seen by many to be synonymous with problem-based learning because both are perceived to be student-centred approaches to learning. Indeed some have argued that they are the same (Boud, 1985). There are others too, who would suggest that problem-based learning can only be undertaken in small groups (Barrows & Tamblyn, 1980), whereas many believe that project-based learning can be undertaken individually, as well as in small groups. Arguably research projects, particularly PhDs, could be said to be the ultimate problem-based approach. However, there are distinct differences between the two approaches, and these are most marked when considering curriculum design rather than in terms of one approach necessarily being more effective than the other. Project-based learning is predominately task-orientated and the project is often set by the tutor. Even if the task or topic is not set, then the parameters and criteria for submission usually are. In terms of the metaverse, projects are often set in VWs or simulations where a team works together on the given project.

Design-based Research

Design-based research has gained considerable attention in the educational research field, particularly in relation to digital technology use. This approach, which blends empirical (e.g. laboratory) research with theory-driven design of learning environments, begins from a positivist standpoint (Brown, 1992). Sandoval and Bell (2004) argued that Brown's early approach to design-based research was an attempt to bridge laboratory studies of learning and studies of complex instructional interventions based on such insights. What was important about Brown's work was the ways in which she illustrated how findings from the laboratory were limited in their ability to explain learning in the classroom, due to the complexity of classroom interactions. Design-based research was developed initially in order to create theories of learning that reflected the complex interaction of diverse learning settings but were created and remain to a large degree located in classical pragmatism. As a result of this, it has been used extensively to design virtual labs and experiments. Examples of this are in areas such as physics and engineering, epitomized in the work of Alves et al. (2022).

Situated Cognition

Situated cognition is where learners are immersed in activities and content that mirrors the situation they are trying to learn about (Brown et al., 1989). Clark and Mayer (2016) extended this by applying the concept of encoding specificity to eLearning. This states that 'transfer [of learning] is maximised when the conditions at retrieval (on the job) match those present at encoding (during learning).' This is based on the observation that the 'transfer of learning back to the job requires that new memories formed during training include the retrieval cues from the job environment.' VR is perhaps ideally suited to creating these cues to encourage later recall. However, some argue that 'the link between the encoding – retrieval match and retention, although generally positive, is essentially correlational rather than causal' (Nairne, 2002). Given the immersive nature of the learning experience through VR, in some contexts, it can be seen as a form of situated cognition. However, there may be exceptions to this; for example, users in VR gathered around a virtual wargames table or a table-sized supermarket model, or just watching a PowerPoint presentation in a virtual classroom. Johnson-Glenberg (2018) discusses the two profound affordances of VR: the sense of presence and the 'embodied affordances of gesture and manipulation in the third dimension [i.e. depth],' and how these enable VR to play a particularly key role in education. She likens these to the Montessori (1966) principles of the importance of movement in learning abstract ideas. Indeed, this also echoes situated learning theory which postulates that the context of learning (i.e. situation and place) is critical to what is learnt (Greeno et al., 1993).

Cognitive Load Theory

Cognitive load theory (Sweller, 1988) is built on the premise that since the brain can only do so many things at once, learning should be defined and focussed. It is based on cognitive studies and the ways in which brains are assumed to store information, for example, that human memory can be divided into working memory and long-term memory, that information is stored in the long-term memory in the form of schemas and that processing new information results in 'cognitive load' on working memory which can affect learning outcomes. In short, cognitive load theory suggests that because short-term memory is limited, learning experiences should be designed to reduce working memory 'load' in order to promote schema acquisition. Recent work in this area related to the metaverse suggests that AR with too much choice can result in too high a cognitive load (Barta et al., 2023).

Actor-Network Theory

Actor-network theory is a means of exploring the relational ties within a network, although it is more of a method than a theory, because it is describing an approach rather than providing explanations for observations. What is central to this approach is that actors may be both human and non-human, thus, for example, supermarket products and digital devices are seen as actors that have influence. Clearly, VR headsets could also be seen as actors if viewed through this lens. Actor-network theory focusses on exploring networks, the impact between networks and actors and the controversies inherent in these. It was originally created by Callon (1986) and Latour (1987) in an attempt to understand processes of technological innovation and scientific knowledge creation. This approach (Latour, 2007) seeks to explain the interaction between the material and the semiotic; semiotics being the study of the ways in which signs and symbols convey meanings in particular ways and thus have an impact on the material world, so in this case, the relationship between things such as symbols, gestures, images and objects and the processes and concepts. However, the approach carries with it a sense of precariousness, since the focus is on nodes/actors that have as many dimensions as connections. Actor-network theory examines the interrelationship and dependence between human meanings and mundane technologies, asking for instance: If there is a growing post-national community emerging in the public-cyber-sphere, then how do nations, national governments and higher education institutions benefit? (Fox, 2005).

Games, Serious Games and Gamification

Games and gamification are approaches to learning that students engage with and to which they are increasingly drawn. There has been much interest in the relationship between games, learning games and serious games. Hamari et al. (2014, p. 3026) defines gamification as the 'process of enhancing services with (motivational) affordances in order to invoke gameful experiences and further behavioural outcomes,' in other words, apply game techniques to non-game environments and activities. In contrast, serious games are complete games whose main purpose is to educate users; they have a clear educational purpose and are not intended to be played primarily for amusement. Markauskaite et al. (2014) provide a comprehensive overview of games for knowledge acquisition, which is perhaps one of the most useful conceptualizations of epistemic games (serious games which encourage a particular way of thinking about a problem) and is summarized as follows:

- *Situated problem-solving games* are played during the investigation and solution of specific professional problems, such as conducting reviews of medications used by patients with multiple diseases in order to identify possible issues, with an aim of proposing better medication plans (pharmacy) or designing lessons for classroom teaching (education).
- *Meta-professional discourse* games are usually played with other professionals within a broader professional field, in order to evaluate various professional products, actions or events. They involve various deconstructions, evaluations and reflections, such as analyses of new medications, evaluations of teaching resources and reflections on one's practices.
- *Translational public discourse games* are played by professionals when they engage in interactions with people who broadly could be described as 'clients.'
- *Weaving games* are played in dynamic action and involve continuous intertwining of meaning-making, social interaction and skilled performance. They range from very specialized games that can require fine-tuned skill – such as strategies for capturing all the spelling mistakes in a literacy test – to quite generic games that require complex coordination of various general and specialized strategies and skills.

This kind of classification of games is helpful in ensuring strong pedagogical foundations, and also indicates the game types which need to be created to compel players to work together; since when individuals become stuck, they are more likely to work collaboratively, as is the case in both well-designed problem-based games, and PBL.

Virtual World Learning

The issues relating to the usability of VWs and the implementation of learning within them are not limited to just any one particular platform. A study by Mavridis et al. (2012) involved a total of 17 participants and compared the OpenSim and *Second Life* platforms to explore how best to exploit them for supporting collaborative learning. The OpenSim platform was evaluated by seven students studying the virtual learning environments module on a postgraduate informatics course through the completion of a self-report questionnaire focussed on functionality, difficulties encountered using the platform and ease of collaboration. The *Second Life* platform was evaluated by ten participants studying the multimedia systems module on an undergraduate informatics course, through a two-phase process. Phase 1 provided researchers with the ability to assess participants' previous knowledge of VWs and individual students the opportunity to become familiar with the VE and associated in-world collaborative tools. During Phase 2, researchers gathered data to assess usability requirements whilst helping facilitate the collaborative activities being undertaken by pairs of students.

The results of their study suggested problems associated with lack of functionality and unfamiliarity with the VW associated with OpenSim were not encountered when the learning tasks were carried out using the *Second Life* platform. In particular, the voice communication features of *Second Life* were fully functional and key to effective collaboration. Based on the results of the study, Mavridis et al. (2012) recommend that VWs for learning need to, firstly, include features that allow application sharing from within the VE to enhance the collaborative functionality of the environment. Secondly, they suggest that for effective collaboration and engagement with PBL in the VW, students should be given the opportunity to become familiar with the VW and in-world collaborative tools over several sessions over an extended period of time. Thirdly, they suggest that efforts should be made to encourage the use of 3D VWs for learning and utilize the skills possessed by students already (e.g. social media tools), thus making the use of such environments more commonplace and increasing students' familiarity with similar tools and environments.

Problem-based Learning in Virtual Worlds

The use and growing recognition of the value of using PBL in virtual words emerged in 2008 and since then it has grown in popularity and diversity of use.

A framework for implementing PBL activities in VEs has been proposed and tested by Vosinakis and Koutsabasis (2012). In their study, ten postgraduate students on a design of interactive and industrial products and systems course were divided into two groups of five to work on a human-computer interface problem focussed on the design of a touch interface for a cafeteria, cinema or theatre for three hours per week over a 12-week period:

- One week for familiarization with technology and the proposed problem.
- Three weeks analyzing the problem through exploration and definition of the problem, and proposing methods for reaching a solution, all results were presented in the VW.
- Five weeks creating potential solutions and prototypes using in-world tools.
- Two weeks evaluating prototypes by students and tutors with feedback and queries in the form of in-world annotations and comments.
- One week presenting group solutions and discussing the knowledge acquired during the problem identification process.

Students' evaluation of the VW PBL activity was generally positive with participants rating (between 0 and 10) their ability to use a number of in-world collaborative tools such as Text Chat (M = 9.3), Projectors (M = 9.0), Message Boards (M = 9.0) and Chat recorders (M = 7.3) favourably. Tools that were less familiar such as Drawing boards (M = 4.0) and Sketch boards (M = 5.8) were rated lower. The results of their study suggest that although VWs can be effective for facilitating PBL activities, successful implementation is more than just designing an appropriate scenario and using a proprietary VW. Their framework suggests three highly related stages that should be followed for creating PBL activities for use in VWs:

- Design an appropriate PBL activity.
- Create a realistic VW environment incorporating appropriate tools to support collaboration and the creation of relevant in-world artefacts.
- Use effective and commensurate evaluation strategies to examine the use of the in-world tools, environment and learning taking place.

Furthermore, they suggest that VWs offer a number of advantages over other online technologies that could be used to facilitate PBL, namely, the ability for all individuals to share and be aware of the progress of other participants in a persistent environment, combined with the ability to customize and adapt their environment and appearance.

An overview of these approaches and references to their current use is provided in Table 3.1.

TABLE 3.1 Learning Online and in the Metaverse

Form of Learning	Original Definitions	Current Examples and Findings
Computer-supported collaborative learning	Initially a branch of the learning sciences concerned with studying how people can learn together with the help of computers.	Jovanović and Milosavljević (2022) developed a high-level software architecture and design for a metaverse platform named VoRtex. VoRtex is primarily designed to support collaborative learning activities with the virtual environment.
Action learning	Action learning was designed to help organizations to develop through problem-solving by asking questions to clarify the exact nature of the problem, reflecting and identifying possible solutions and only then taking action.	Ellis and Phelps (2000) created a collaborative action learning model which is described as a vehicle for staff development and change management so that staff make the transition to online teachers or learning facilitators.
Problem-orientated learning	This form of learning focusses on the idea that when asking students to solve problems, some knowledge is more foundational than other knowledge and should necessarily be taught first.	Gao et al. (2015) investigated problem-oriented learning in online learning environments. The study compared the impact of knowledge map representation with traditional hierarchical representation. Participants who used the knowledge map representation had better problem-solving performance.
Project-based learning	Project-based learning is predominately task orientated and the project is often set by the tutor.	Hou et al. (2023) constructed a pedagogical model for teaching and learning activities of a university's hospitality and real-estate programme. The study found that the VR-aided and project-based pedagogy model is novel and effective in delivering green building education.
Design-based research	This is an approach which blends research with theory-driven design of learning environments.	Hoadley and Campos (2022) argue that both research and design can independently produce empirically derived knowledge and discuss how research (DBR) methods contribute various types of usable knowledge that can not only produce better online interventions but also transform people and systems.
Situated cognition	Situated cognition is where learners are immersed in activities and content that mirrors the situation they are trying to learn about.	Chylinski et al. (2020) used situated cognition theories and developed a framework of Augmented Reality Marketing experiences to synthesize current research and applications.

(Continued)

TABLE 3.1 (Continued)

Form of Learning	Original Definitions	Current Examples and Findings
Cognitive load theory	This theory suggests that because short-term memory is limited, learning experiences should be designed to reduce working memory 'load' in order to promote schema acquisition.	Barta et al. (2023) undertook research that examined the effects that augmented reality had on cognitive variables related to cognitive load. The results showed that AR reduces cognitive dissonance through its effects on perceived similarity and confusion caused by overchoice. Furthermore, lower cognitive load enhanced shopping purchase intentions, resulting in greater willingness to pay more for the product.
Actor-network theory	This focusses on exploring both networks, and the impact between networks and actors, and the controversies inherent in these.	Söderholm et al. (2019) analysed the roles policies, so-called network management, throughout the entire technological development processes. The paper provides an analytical framework that addresses the changing roles of network management at the interface between various phases of the technological development process.
Games and gamification	This is the application of game techniques to non-game environments and activities. However, serious games are those whose main purpose is to educate users; they have a clear educational purpose and are not intended to be played primarily for amusement.	Thomas et al. (2023) conducted interviews with experienced gamification designers from different industries and parts of the world. The findings indicate that gamification is influenced by positive psychology and the metaverse.
Virtual world learning	Learning in VWs means students can interact and learn in 3D graphical online environments and can work on specifically tailored or self-developed projects.	Wang et al. (2020) synthesized the research findings of the impact of VW learning on language learning. The meta-analysis showed significant overall linguistic and affective gains.
Problem-based learning in VWs	This is the use of PBL – where students work in small teams to analyze and manage a problem presented to them, in a VW such as *Second Life* or Unity3D where they can work collaboratively.	Davis et al. (2016) evaluated a simulated clinical practice opportunity using web-based platforms. The findings indicated that students became more aware of the role of the other healthcare professionals involved and found the VWs to be realistic and useful, which in turn contributed to their engagement with the scenario provided.

Conclusion

Whilst learning in the metaverse, still, at one level, appears relatively new, it is clear that this is not the case. Learning in the metaverse has, in many ways, been in existence since the advent of the internet. However, although most staff have become familiar with using virtual learning environments for learning, linking the metaverse into effective learning and teaching still appears to be troublesome. Yet by repurposing and redesigning learning spaces in the metaverse in innovative ways then it will be possible to enable more flexible uses and diverse purposes in ways that will enhance learning. In terms of the development of theories and pedagogies, in some respects, learning in the metaverse presents what appear to be a unique set of challenges, but in fact, it could be argued that these mirror the persistent questions around which higher education research and development constantly revolve and evolve, some of which will be discussed in Chapter 4.

References

Alves, G. R., Marques, M. A., Fidalgo, A. V., García-Zubía, J., Castro, M., Hernández-Jayo, U., García-Loro, F., & Kreiter, C. (2022). A roadmap for the VISIR remote lab. *European Journal of Engineering Education, 48*(5), 880–898.

Barrows, H. S., & Tamblyn, R. M. (1980). *Problem-based learning: An approach to medical education* (Vol. 1). Springer Publishing Company.

Barta, S., Gurrea, R., & Flavián, C. (2023). Using augmented reality to reduce cognitive dissonance and increase purchase intention. *Computers in Human Behavior, 140,* 107564. https://doi.org/10.1016/j.chb.2022.107564

Benford, S. (2009). Hybrid spatial structures in ubiquitous computing, Paper for the *Bigraphs Workshop.*

Bloom, B. S. (1956). Taxonomy of educational objectives: The classification of educational goals. In M. D. Engelhart, E. J. Furs, W. H. Hill, & D. R. Krathwohl (Eds.), *Taxonomy of educational objectives: The classification of educational goals; Handbook I: Cognitive domain* (1st ed.). Longman Group.

Boud, D. (1985). Introduction. In D. Boud (Ed.), *Problem-based learning in education for the professions* (pp. 5–13). HERDSA.

Brown, A. L. (1992). Design experiments: Theoretical and methodological challenges in creating complex interventions in classroom settings. *The Journal of the Learning Sciences, 2*(2), 141–178.

Brown, J. S., Collins, A., & Duguid, P. (1989). Situated cognition and the culture of learning. *Educational Researcher, 18*(1), 32–42.

Callon, M. (1986). The sociology of an actor-network: The case of the electric vehicle. In J. Lawand, & A. Rip (Eds.), *Mapping the dynamics of science and technology* (pp. 19–34). Macmillan.

Chylinski, M., Heller, J., Hilken, T., Keeling, D. I., Mahr, D., & de Ruyter, K. (2020). Augmented reality marketing: A technology-enabled approach to situated customer experience. *Australasian Marketing Journal*, *28*(4), 374–384. https://doi.org/10.1016/j.ausmj.2020.04.004

Clark, R. C., & Mayer, R. E. (2016). *E-learning and the science of instruction: Proven guidelines for consumers and designers of multimedia learning*. John Wiley & sons.

Dalgarno, B., & Lee, M. J. W. (2010). What are the learning affordances of 3-D virtual environments? *British Journal of Educational Technology*, *41*(1), 10–32.

Davis, D. L., Hercelinskyj, G., & Jackson, L. M. (2016). Promoting interprofessional collaboration: A pilot project using simulation in the virtual world of Second Life. *Journal of Research in Interprofessional Practice and Education*, *6*(2), 1–15.

Ellis, A., & Phelps, R. (2000). Staff development for online delivery: A collaborative, team based action learning model. *Australasian Journal of Educational Technology*, *16*(1), 26–44.

Fowler, C. (2015). Learning activities in 3-D virtual worlds. *British Journal of Educational Technology*, *46*, 412–422.

Fox, S. (2005). An actor-network critique of community in higher education: Implications for networked learning. *Studies in Higher Education*, *30*(1), 95–110.

Gao, Q., Wang, D., & Gao, F. (2015). Impact of knowledge representations on problem-oriented learning in online environments. *International Journal of Human–Computer Interaction*, *31*(12), 922–938. https://doi.org/10.1080/10447318.2015.1072788

Greeno, J. G., Moore, J. L., & Smith, D. R. (1993). Transfer of situated learning. In D. K. Detterman, & R. J. Sternberg (Eds.), *Transfer on trial: Intelligence, cognition, and instruction* (pp. 99–167). Ablex Publishing.

Hamari, J., Koivisto, J., & Sarsa, H. (2014). Does gamification work?–A literature review of empirical studies on gamification. *2014 47th Hawaii International Conference on System Sciences*, 3025–3034.

Hoadley, C., & Campos, F. C. (2022). Design-based research: What it is and why it matters to studying online learning. *Educational Psychologist*, *57*(3), 207–220.

Hou, H., Lai, J. H. K., & Wu, H. (2023). Project-based learning and pedagogies for virtual reality-aided green building education: Case study on a university course. *International Journal of Sustainability in Higher Education*, *24*(6), 1308–1327.

Hwang, G. J., & Chien, S. Y. (2022). Definition, roles, and potential research issues of the metaverse in education: An artificial intelligence perspective. *Computers and Education: Artificial Intelligence*, *3*. https://doi.org/10.1016/j.caeai.2022.100082

Johnson-Glenberg, M. C. (2018). Immersive VR and education: Embodied design principles that include gesture and hand controls. *Frontiers in Robotics and AI*, *5*, 81.

Jovanović, A., & Milosavljević, A. (2022). VoRtex metaverse platform for gamified collaborative learning. *Electronics*, *11*(3), 317.

Latour, B. (1987). *Science in action: How to follow scientists and engineers through society*. Open University Press.

Latour, B. (2007). *Reassembling the social: An introduction to actor-network-theory*. Oxford University Press.

Lee, L.-H., Braud, T., Zhou, P., Wang, L., Xu, D., Lin, Z., Kumar, A., Bermejo, C., & Hui, P. (2021). All one needs to know about metaverse: A complete survey on technological singularity, virtual ecosystem, and research agenda. *ArXiv Preprint ArXiv:2110.05352*.

Loke, S.-K. (2015). How do virtual world experiences bring about learning? A critical review of theories. *Australasian Journal of Educational Technology, 31*(1), 112–122.

Margetson, D. (1991). Why is problem-based learning a challenge? In D. Boud & G. Feletti (Eds.), *The challenge of problem-based learning* (pp. 36–44). Kogan Page.

Markauskaite, L., Goodyear, P., & Bachfischer, A. (2014). Epistemic games for knowledgeable action in professional learning. *ICLS 2014 Symposium: Enrollment of Higher Education Students in Professional Knowledge and Practices, Boulder, CO, 23*, 27.

Mavridis, A., Konstantinidis, A., & Tsiatsos, T. (2012). A comparison of 3D collaborative virtual learning environments: OpenSim vs. Second Life. *International Journal of E-Collaboration (IJeC), 8*(4), 8–21.

McConnell, D. (2006). *E-learning groups and communities*. SRHE/Open University Press.

McGill, I., & Beaty, L. (2001). *Action learning: A guide for professional, management & educational development* (2nd ed.). Kogan Page.

Mikropoulos, T. A., & Natsis, A. (2011). Educational virtual environments: A ten-year review of empirical research (1999–2009). *Computers & Education, 56*(3), 769–780.

Milgram, P., & Kishino, F. (1994). A taxonomy of mixed reality visual displays. *IEICE TRANSACTIONS on Information and Systems, 77*(12), 1321–1329.

Montessori, M. (1966). *The secret of childhood*. Ballantine Books.

Nairne, J. S. (2002). The myth of the encoding-retrieval match. *Memory, 10*(5–6), 389–395.

Narin, N. G. (2021). Journal of metaverse a content analysis of the metaverse articles. *Journal of Metaverse*, 17–24. www.secondlife.com

Ning, H., Wang, H., Lin, Y., Wang, W., Dhelim, S., Farha, F., Ding, J., & Daneshmand, M. (2021). A survey on metaverse: The state-of-the-art, technologies, applications, and challenges. *ArXiv Preprint ArXiv:2111.09673.*

Resnick, L. B. (1991). Shared cognition: Thinking as social practice. In L. B. Resnick, J. M. Levine, & S. D. Teasley (Eds.), *Perspectives on socially shared cognition* (pp. 1–20). American Psychological Association.

Roschelle, J., & Teasley, S. (1995). The construction of shared knowledge in collaborative problem solving. In C. E. O'Malley (Ed.), *Computer supported collaborative learning* (pp. 69–97). Springer-Verlag.

Sandoval, W. A., & Bell, P. (2004). Design-based research methods for studying learning in context: Introduction. *Educational Psychologist, 39*(4), 199–201.

Schott, C., & Marshall, S. (2021). Virtual reality for experiential education: A user experience exploration. *Australasian Journal of Educational Technology, 37*(1), 96–110.

Söderholm, P., Hellsmark, H., Frishammar, J., Hansson, J., Mossberg, J., & Sandström, A. (2019). Technological development for sustainability: The role of network management in the innovation policy mix. *Technological Forecasting and Social Change, 138*, 309–323. https://doi.org/10.1016/j.techfore.2018.10.010

Sweller, J. (1988). Cognitive load during problem solving: Effects on learning. *Cognitive Science, 12*(2), 257–285.

Thomas, N. J., Baral, R., Crocco, O. S., & Mohanan, S. (2023). A framework for gamification in the metaverse era: How designers envision gameful experience. *Technological Forecasting and Social Change, 193*, 122544. https://doi.org/10.1016/j.techfore.2023.122544

Tlili, A., Huang, R., Shehata, B., Liu, D., Zhao, J., Metwally, A. H. S., Wang, H., Denden, M., Bozkurt, A., Lee, L. H., Beyoglu, D., Altinay, F., Sharma, R. C., Altinay, Z., Li, Z., Liu, J., Ahmad, F., Hu, Y., Salha, S., … Burgos, D. (2022). Is metaverse in education a blessing or a curse: A combined content and bibliometric analysis. In *Smart learning environments* (Vol. 9, Issue 1). Springer. https://doi.org/10.1186/s40561-022-00205-x

Vosinakis, S., & Koutsabasis, P. (2012). Problem-based learning for design and engineering activities in virtual worlds. *PRESENCE: Teleoperators and Virtual Environments*, *21*(3), 338–358.

Wang, C., Lan, Y.-J., Tseng, W.-T., Lin, Y.-T. R., & Gupta, K. C.-L. (2020). On the effects of 3D virtual worlds in language learning – A meta-analysis. *Computer Assisted Language Learning*, *33*(8), 891–915. https://doi.org/10.1080/09588221.2019.1598444

4

Rethinking Pedagogy for the Metaverse

Introduction

This chapter will consider the impact of advances in technology on pedagogy and the increasing use of learning online. It begins by examining the stances and experiences of learners in the metaverse, drawing on both older and more recent research. The importance of the stances model of learning is that it offers an alternative view of student learning from the standardized model of learning styles. The chapter then explores some of the particular areas of value when using the metaverse, including the value of the visual, the value of learning spaces, the value of openness and the value of experiential opportunities. The final section of the chapter examines the broader impact of the metaverse on higher education and suggests that pedagogy needs to be re-examined in the light of the metaverse.

Learners in the Metaverse: Exploring Learning Stances

Whilst the model of learning stances presented below could, at first, be seen as being overly straightforward, it not only represents learners and teachers as having more than one style but also a spatial locale from which they operate. Learning in the metaverse means that students need to understand their stance and the ways it affects their learning in different times and spaces. Furthermore, staff stances affect the way in which they design learning for the metaverse and this needs to be recognized. The model of learning stances presented below captures the complexity of learning as an individual and with others, as well as locating one's own view of pedagogy – which invariably changes according to location and learning space. This model also links well with White and Le Cornu's (2017) notion of engagement genres.

DOI: 10.1201/9781003413875-5

Learning Stances

It is suggested here that instead of adopting generalized conceptions of learning or learning styles it is vital that learning is located with/in the identities of the learner. Since the early 2000s, there has been increasing debate about the value of learning styles, although as an idea they do remain popular with many in staff development, business communities and the military. To move away from the idea of learning styles removes possibilities for generalizing learner approaches and instead presents the notion that learning is complex and specific to the learner and must therefore be located in the context of their lives and their stories.

The notion of stance is used here to indicate that students, at different times and in different spaces, 'locate' themselves as individual learners. To some extent, stances in and towards learning are invariably formulated through school experiences and parental expectations. However, this model of learning stances (Savin-Baden, 2000) stands against the notion of learning styles, and holist and serialist, deep and surface approaches to learning, arguing instead that stances relate not only to cognitive perspectives but also to ontological positioning within learning environments. Conflict between expectation, identity and belief in a learning context can result in staff and students becoming stuck: experiencing disjunction in learning and teaching, either personally, pedagogically or interactionally.

Stance is used here in the sense of one's attitude, belief or disposition towards a particular context, person or experience. It refers to a particular position one takes up in life towards something, at a particular point in time. Stance is not just a matter of attitude; it encompasses our unconscious beliefs and prejudices, our prior learning experiences, our perceptions of tutors, peers and learning situations and our past, present and future selves. Each stance contains a number of domains and movement between them is diverse, depending on each individual and set of circumstances. The borders of the domains are somewhat blurred, as in the edges of colours in the spectrum. Movement can also take place within domains as well as across them. The stances are defined briefly as follows (Figure 4.1):

- Personal stance: the way in which staff and students see themselves in relation to the learning context and give their own distinctive meaning to their experience of that context.
- Pedagogical stance: the ways in which people see themselves as learners in particular educational environments.
- Interactional stance: the ways in which learners work and learn in groups and construct meaning in relation to one another.

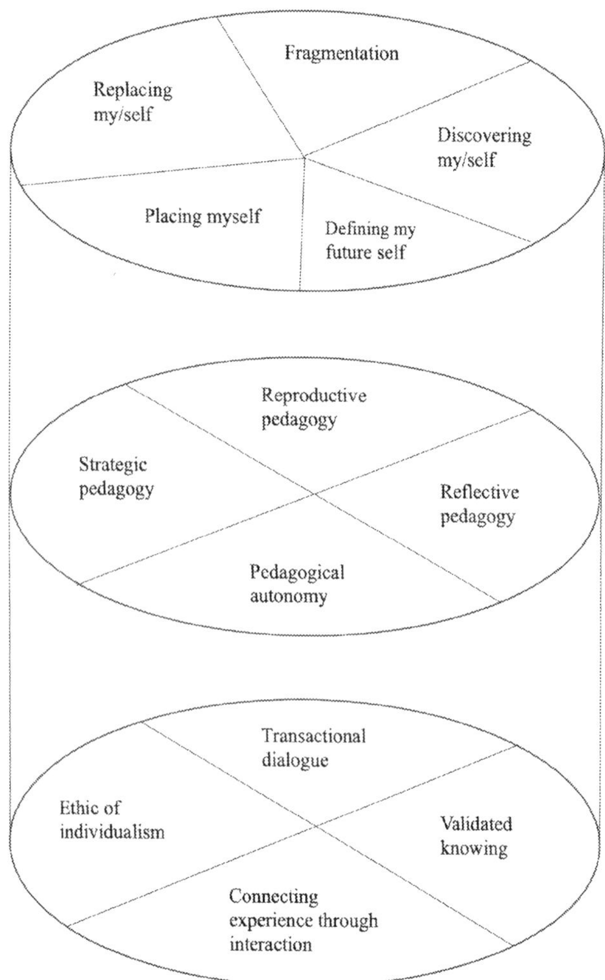

FIGURE 4.1 Learning stances.

The domains within Personal stance are as follows:

Fragmentation
Students in this domain of personal stance experience challenges to their values and beliefs which they then consider to be at risk or are threatened through these challenges and the arising uncertainty.

Discovering myself
In this domain, students experience self-validation through learning that promotes a reflexive search for self-knowledge and self-improvement.

Defining my future self
The concept of defining themselves relates to students positioning themselves in the learning context in terms of their view of themselves as future professionals, which, in turn, governs the possibilities and limits of engagement with the material, the context and other people.

Placing myself in relation to my life-world
Through placing themselves, students gain a heightened understanding of their own reality because of the way in which learning challenges them to confront the relationship between the previous experiences of their life-world (Husserl, 1907/1964) and their new learning experiences.

Re-placing myself: knowing the world differently
The notion of 'knowing the world differently' captures the idea that students are able to frame their learning experiences for themselves and simultaneously challenge the institutions and sociopolitical contexts in which they live, work and learn. Students within this domain are able to take up alternative perspectives in order to challenge both themselves and the world.

The next stance, pedagogical stance, depicts the way in which students see themselves as learners in particular educational environments. The four domains within this stance are presented as follows:

Reproductive pedagogy
Learning, for these students, is expected to be safe and predictable, requiring neither personal initiative nor critical thought. Tutors are seen to be the suppliers of all legitimate knowledge, since anything less will result in risk and failure for the students and tutors will be perceived by the students to be inefficient.

Strategic pedagogy
Students in this domain may use several different learning strategies, but these are all within the remit of what is acceptable to both the authorities (institution, staff and profession) and the student. Here pedagogical stance is characterized by a form of cue-seeking through which students seek out cues in order to pass assessments.

Pedagogical autonomy
Students here adopt a position of learning which they perceive will offer them the greatest degree of autonomy. Students opt to learn in a way that suits them and that will offer them, as far as they are concerned, the most effective means of learning, meeting their own personally defined needs as learners yet also ensuring that they will pass the course.

Reflective pedagogy
Reflective pedagogy encompasses the notion that students see learning and knowledge as flexible entities. Students within this domain perceive that there are also other valid ways of seeing things besides their own perspective, and they accept that all kinds of knowing can help them to 'know' the world better. This domain is characterized by evaluating personal and propositional knowledge on one's own terms; thus, the student both engages with knowledge and also questions it.

Staff stances are also important here in terms designing learning in the metaverse and are described as follows:

- *Reproductive pedagogy* staff see themselves as the suppliers of all legitimate knowledge and therefore as facilitators they act as gap fillers.
- *Strategic pedagogy* staff employ tactics that prompt students' cue-seeking behaviour.
- *Pedagogical autonomy* staff enable students to meet their own personally defined needs as learners while also ensuring that they will pass the course.
- *Reflective pedagogy* staff help students to realize that learning is a flexible entity and that there are also other valid ways of seeing things besides their own perspective.

The final stance, interactional stance, captures the ways in which learners work and learn in groups and construct meaning in relation to one another.

The ethic of individualism
The 'ethic of individualism' (Lukes, 1973) depicts the notion that some students see learning within the group as an activity that is only valuable in terms of what they as an individual could gain from it. These students place little value upon collective learning experiences and are more concerned that they may forego marks by expending effort sharing tasks and information within the group rather than if they worked alone.

Validated knowing through 'real talk'
The domain captures the idea that through the experience of being heard within a group, and being valued by other group members, individual students learn to value their own knowledge and experience. Being in this domain enables students to come to value their personal and propositional knowledge by recognizing its value through the perspectives of others.

Connecting experience through interaction
This domain is characterized by the individual being facilitated through the group process in making sense, through reflection, of their own reality and in confronting dilemmas and problems within that reality. Thus, in this domain, students use the group to make sense of their world as it appears to be and will use the group to resolve dilemmas and discover meaning in their lives.

Transactional dialogue: mediating different worlds
Transactional dialogue (after Brookfield, 1985) is used here to capture the idea that the group serves as an interactive function for the individual. Through the group, the individual is enabled to learn both through the experience of others and the appreciation of other people's life-worlds, and by reflecting upon these, to relate them to their own.

It is important to note that the borders of the domains merge with one another, and therefore shifts between domains represent transitional areas where particular kinds of transitional learning and teaching occur.

These stances can be linked to the metaphor of visitors and residents as defined by White and Le Cornu (2011). For example, students who have a fragmented personal stance and adopt reproductive pedagogy are more likely to be a visitor; students who value connection, transactional dialogue and reflective pedagogy are more likely to be residents. For example, visitors use the web to undertake particular tasks which have some concrete benefit and are unlikely to have any form of online profile. Visitors see the web as something to achieve particular goals such as ordering books, finding information or emailing someone. Residents live parts of their lives online and the distinction between online and offline is increasingly blurred; they have a social networking profile and see the web as a place to express opinions, and undertake useful activities such as online banking, shopping and networked learning. For residents, value is seen in terms of networking and interaction, as well as a source of knowledge. They live out much of their life online, visitors do not. This metaphor of visitors and residents captures the ways in which people's online engagement can be conceptualized; they argue

> Visitors and Residents mapping does, in part, make our online lives and motivations visible in a form which can be reflected upon and discussed with a human, rather than technocentric, focus. It operates on a miso level contextualising the motivations of individuals and groups within socioeconomic or institutional frames.
>
> **(White and Le Cornu, 2011)**

The idea of visitors and residents in the context of learning illustrates both the relationship with pedagogy and the need for belonging and community, as White's Figure 4.2 illustrates.

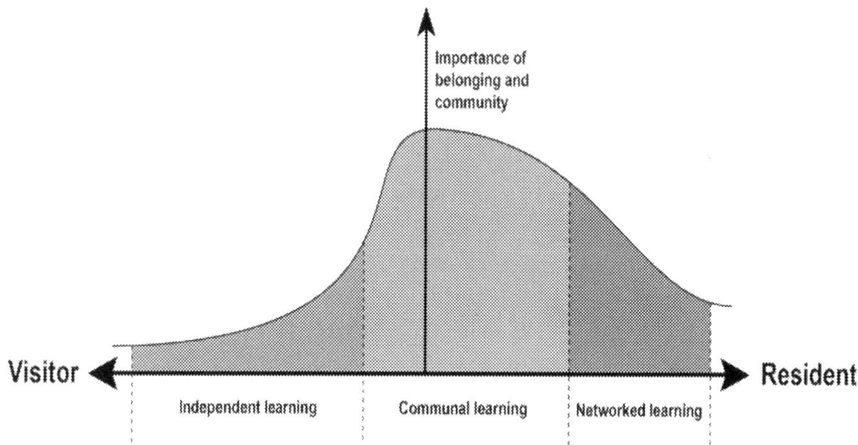

FIGURE 4.2 Visitors and residents continuum (reproduced with permission).

White's model of spatiality is also useful in understanding students' stances. He suggests that spatial collaboration is stronger when we are co-present in buildings but that this copresence and connectedness is often lacking in the online environment. It is clear too that the visual is also important when considering pedagogy for the metaverse.

The Value of the Visual

Higher education has moved from blackboard and chalk, through overhead projectors and flip charts on to PowerPoint, and this, together with society's increasing use of television and computer games, has resulted in a culture that increasingly focusses on the visual. Accounts from staff and students would seem to indicate that many university students use social networking (such as Twitter and Facebook) rather than communicate via the university virtual learning environment. Although this does not account for the use of the metaverse, what it does shed light on is the value of social networking for learning, something which higher education should perhaps capitalize on more than it currently does so.

While the (often) ordered university virtual learning environments still continue (such as Blackboard), and indeed were considered innovative in their day, immersive spaces such as the metaverse offer a visual experience, and a sense of 'being' in a learning space in ways that managed learning systems do not. Even if this very visuality may not be vital for students on face-to-face courses, it does appear to help those on distance programmes to feel more engaged with peers and what is being learned on the course. Whether it is learning to build, or learning through discussion, the metaverse also seems to help students to build a learning community. Perhaps this is due to the fact that the metaverse is a synchronous learning space and therefore its immediacy brings with it a perspective of being and learning with others in a way that other asynchronous forms of learning do not.

The value of the visual nature of the metaverse is in the ability to use it for learning in visual ways not possible in real life. For example, it is possible to build houses that replicate real-life homes in which occupational therapists can evaluate whether the house is suitable for a patient to return to following a hip replacement. It is possible to create a crime scene where police students can consider how to take photographs and understand the importance of not contaminating it. These exemplars might seem little more than basic simulation, but they are ones that staff and students themselves can design and build – with the help of a learning technologist, and then adapt over time. A recent example is the work of Poyade et al. (2019) who used extended reality to create user-centric learning of anatomy. The authors used virtual reality and augmented reality in a taught master's degree in medical visualization and human anatomy which combined cadaveric dissection and interactive visualization techniques.

Disciplines shape the nature of pedagogy, and such pedagogies reflect the practices and culture of the discipline. Yet it is not just the visual nature of metaverse that is appealing; it is also the learning spaces it offers.

The Value of Learning Spaces

There is an increasing interest in the notion of space and the design of physical space, and the use of the metaverse is consistent with increased attention being directed at socio-material perspectives on learning. Early work by Temple (2008) reviewed research into the built environment of universities, linking this to the organizational nature of higher education in terms of how universities are governed and managed, including changing relations with their students, research relating to how students learn and factors influencing the learning process. He developed a useful agenda for future research, much of which still remains to be done. More recent contributions to this discourse have emphasized evolving space usage, the importance of spaces that can be used flexibly and alignment between space and the curriculum (Beckers et al., 2015; Nordquist et al., 2016). As a counterbalance, Thomas challenges the dominance of physical spaces in the discourse about space and learning. He argues that there is little recognition that our conceptions of learning are bounded by the 'physical situatedness' of learning itself, creating unhelpful and inadequately challenged distinctions between conceptions of learning in different types of space, such as classrooms, libraries, cafes, clinical areas and online (Thomas, 2010). There has been relatively little consideration of space as a site of learning and more particularly as a site of power. Kitto et al. (2013) argued that space and place are underconceptualized in the health professions' literature. Nordquist et al. (2013) provide a commentary on articles that address the impact of learning spaces in professional education. The authors discourage designing physical learning spaces based on specific educational methods but instead encourage the design of flexible hybrid spaces for learning, that can remain relevant as learning and teaching changes. They advocate strengthening the alignment between the curriculum and space provision through sequential consideration of:

- The vision of the curriculum: an exploration of the need for and type of formal and informal spaces;
- Existing spaces and an analysis of how these might be classified and;
- The gap between the vision and what existing spaces provide, to guide redevelopment or creation of new learning spaces.

This is less radical than Thomas's vision of blurred distinction between physical and online spaces for learning, since these increasingly meld together in a learner's multifaceted learning experiences, and it is difficult to articulate 'where' particular learning occurs. Thomas (2010) also calls for learning spaces to be designed as adaptive, malleable and enchanting spaces which provide opportunities for emergent types of learning. Moving beyond the discourses of physical and virtual learning spaces, Savin-Baden (2008) argues for the need to see spaces between people and places in terms of:

- Territorial spaces between the tribes of academia, whether disciplinary, professional, or departmental. These are places in which understandings about issues of power, status, and emphasis are important.
- Space between learner and teacher: the concerns and agendas of learners and teachers are different spaces with diverse emphases, and such spaces are often complex and difficult to manage. Often, these spaces are not just different in territory but also in language and social practices. (p. 10–11)

The challenge of creating effective learning spaces in the metaverse is an ongoing challenge, which brings with it the need to value openness.

The Value of Openness

The metaverse is an environment that can be used freely, and the ability just to use an interesting space to provide learning in a visual environment is appealing. This is because it brings a sense of freedom from the often bounded university systems and restrictions. In the metaverse, it is not necessary to book a room and it is relatively easy to find or create space not normally used for teaching, such as a virtual wild space or a beach. It seems that its very openness and flexibility is something that staff not only value for teaching but also use for socializing. This openness too seems to bring with it a sense of freedom to think differently about teaching and learning but it also offers opportunities to try out new and different activities. Staff often speak of it as a space that is more like the bar; it is a social medium where informality, ingenuity and wit are valued. However, there is also a recognition that such openness brings challenges, so that metaverse is seen as an open but somewhat divided culture where the creative and the materialistic sides of the space could be seen to vie with one another. It is a creative and experimental space and, in many ways, might be seen as a 'third space.' The notion of the 'third space' captures the idea that there are 'particular discursive spaces … in which alternative and competing discourses and positioning transform conflict and difference into rich zones of collaboration and learning' (Gutiérrez et al., 1999, pp. 286–287). The metaverse provides a discursive space, a space in which changing spaces, experimenting and learning differently creates a polycontextual space, which for some staff will offer a move away from performativity.

This kind of openness to learning and teaching offered by the metaverse largely reflects critical awareness theories of learning whereby learning shapes people in such a profound way that it affects all subsequent learning (Freire, 1972, 1974; Mezirow, 1981) as well as dialogic learning. Yet it is also a space that seems to encourage the use of dialogic learning. Dialogic learning encourages students to draw upon their own experience to explain the concepts and ideas with which they are presented, and then use that experience to make sense for themselves and also to explore further issues. Dialogue brings to the fore, for students and tutors, the value of prior experience to current learning and thus can engage them in explorations and (re)constructions of their beliefs about learning and ways of valuing the experiential.

The Value of Experiential Opportunities

For many staff, the initial rationale for using the metaverse in higher education is because practicing skills within a virtual environment online offers advantages over learning through real-life practice, in particular, the exposure of learners to a wide range of scenarios (more than they are likely to meet in a standard face-to-face programme) at a time and pace convenient to the learner, together with consistent feedback. Such experiential practices are increasingly seen as important when the opportunity to try out learning and explore practice are increasingly limited for students being educated for the professions. It also offers learners the chance to make mistakes without real-world repercussions.

With the increasing use of distance programmes, the metaverse creates online learning opportunities which are sufficiently immersive and collaborative outside the tutorial room, in ways that some managed learning systems do not. However, what is also important to note is the way in which the metaverse enables learners both to relate strongly to real-life experiences and also to focus on the importance of learning *with* and *through* experience. Dewey (1938) emphasized the human capacity to reconstruct experience and thus make meaning of it and suggested that education should be seen as a process of continuous reconstruction and growth of experience. He believed that the role of the teacher was to organize learning activities which built on the previous experiences of the students and direct them to new experiences that furthered their growth. Thus, the curriculum should be closely tied to the students' experiences, developmentally appropriate and structured in ways that foster continuity. Learning with and through others, and across networks, with peers and through exploration and experimentation, is vital in creating and re-envisioning pedagogies for the metaverse.

The Metaverse as a Mirror on Higher Education Practices

The use of the metaverse in higher education has created a stir in some quarters for a whole raft of reasons – mostly around purpose, pedagogy and ethics. However, such questioning has then prompted further queries being raised about teaching and learning in general. For example, concerns about the use of metaverse have resulted in questions being asked about why subjects are taught in particular ways, how teaching can be adapted and how learning can be improved. It is also important to consider the relationship between the use of metaverse and the subject or discipline in which it is being used. There has been increasing discussion about discipline-based pedagogy worldwide. Disciplinary teaching and learning habits were explored in the work of Shulman (2005) in his research on signature pedagogies. Here, he explains signature pedagogies as 'the forms of instruction that leap to mind when we first think about the preparation of members for a particular profession,' illustrating that the students are taught to think, perform and act with integrity (2005, p. 52). It is noteworthy that Shulman's work is professionally focussed, and the disciplines included in his study are, therefore, more strongly associated with applied knowledge, such as medicine and law. However, other researchers have extended the use of the concept of 'signature pedagogies' by exploring the teaching and learning habits of disciplinary groups that have not routinely been considered to be professional groups (Chick et al., 2011). Thus, in discussions about the use of metaverse within the curriculum, it is important to consider the way in which disciplines themselves shape the teaching and learning practices belief systems. For example, teacher knowledge and beliefs about what to do, how to do it and under which circumstances can affect the way that students learn a particular subject matter. Furthermore, it is also important to recognize that what works well and effectively the first time may not do so subsequently, and vice versa. Perhaps what is also important then when deciding to use the metaverse is to differentiate between reasons for adopting the metaverse, such as activities that cannot be done in real life, or reasons for using it instead of something else, for example, instead of a discussion forum.

The introduction of the metaverse has also raised questions about the institutional power and control of learning. This might be reflected in who controls the university metaverse or what is allowed or disallowed in that space, as well as what is and is not acceptable practice. A range of questions are being asked by academics about why we might want to learn in such a space and whether learning through an avatar or virtual reality is really any better than learning through discussion boards. Developing learning in the metaverse therefore introduces a challenge about how we design curricula, and how we can design them for more process-based approaches to learning, and in particular, social learning. In short, it holds up a mirror to current pedagogies and practices in higher education and helps us to consider why and how we do what we do. Hudson-Smith (2022) argues, in the context of urban planning

> The metaverse is, at first sight, a mirror to the current world, a digital twin, but it is more than this: It is an inhabited mirror world where the physical dimensions and rules of time and space do not necessarily apply. Operating across scales, from the change of use of a building up to a local plan and onwards to the scale of future cities, these emerging metaverses will exist either directly within computational space or emerge into our physical space via augmented reality. (p. 343)

Future university buildings, physical and virtual, need to be considered when designing pedagogy for the metaverse, since as yet there remains relatively little in-depth pedagogical design that is able to inform the evolving challenge and nature of the metaverse. It is also important to recognize that there is still comparatively little research worldwide about what does and does not work effectively in the metaverse. Whilst evidence is mounting and much of what is discussed is shared practice, relatively few new pedagogical models have emerged, and theorization is only just beginning. Savin-Baden (2023) suggests what needs to occur is the unsettlement of university spaces through seven fluid pillars for a changing postdigital university, namely:

Academic Freedom

The university needs to (re)embrace the idea that it should create space for unconditional engagement that explores diverse truth and celebrates space where controversy and debate are highly valued. The university should not be a space where cancel culture exists or where silence is used as a weapon.

Valuing Silence and Slowness

Carvalho and Diogo (2021) have reflected that clock time has always been an instrument of social control and suggest that clock time is used as a management tool to rule personal time as well as professional time. The idea of slow space is not just a rejection of being busy but a realization of the need for slowness amidst the busyness. Such spaces could include writing spaces and designated tech-free silent spaces.

Spaces of Critical Thought

The underlying purpose of education and educators is to 'develop the capacities to think critically … to understand oneself critically and to act critically, thereby forming critical persons who are not subject to the world, but able to act autonomously and purposively within it' (Barnett, 1997, p. 7). However, in the context of a neoliberal system, this requires thinking spaces. Thinking spaces are defined here as opportunities to take a view, to reflect on some closely read article or to consider a lecture which has been attended.

Universities as Spaces for Life

The idea of the university as a space for life 'is configured as a simultaneous dwelling-in and spacing-out, where the "out" also implies a *trans-* as in transition, transformation and transgression' (Arndt et al., 2020, p. 254). The idea, then, is that the university offers spaces for thinking, for events and even outside quiet spaces in which to be away from the busyness of life.

Environmental Activism

The largest problem remains CO_2 emissions and the burning of fossil fuels. Boden et al. (2010) suggested that whilst there has been some levelling off as rich countries, such as the United States and the United Kingdom, have cut their emissions, other countries such as China and India have not. One of the main difficulties that universities face is that even those researching climate change, such as the University of Oxford, are funded by the petrochemical industry. Hodson (2021) argues that universities need to be brave enough to take a stance against funding from the fossil fuel industry.

Radical Dissent

The idea of radical dissent is seen as a prompt for change. Academics who seek such change, who question or who express diverse or alternative views are catalysts for new ideas and new approaches to learning. This may appear to be a subversion, something that is looked on unfavourably, but in fact this is to misunderstand what it means to subvert. As Davids (2021) notes, disagreement and dissent should be at the heart of the university ethos, indicating that conflicting truths have a right to be heard.

Seeking Truths

There is considerable suggestion in the 21st-century university that we are in an era of post-truth. However, the difficulty with the term post-truth is that it is often used in conjunction with terms such as fake news and misinformation, as well as political disinformation spread through social media. Human beings are really human be(com)ings constituted in the play of language. Too often we use language to declare, assert, prove, argue, convince and proclaim notions of 'truth.' Yet what happens when we emphasize the use of language to question, play with, savour and ruminate on notions of 'truth' or truths? The language of collaboration invites conversation, and a keen sense of confidence that we are engaging together in creating intellectual, emotional, spiritual and aesthetic possibilities.

Such fluid pillars will enable the university and other institutional learning spaces to adapt to the metaverse and create innovative pedagogies for a postdigital age.

Conclusion

This chapter has argued that pedagogies need to be rethought for the metaverse. Traditional lectures and seminar-based models of learning in physical space are not entirely redundant but they are often not a good fit with new forms of learning emerging in the metaverse. What is needed is a recognition that learning stances and learning spaces are fluid. Pedagogy for the metaverse must be seen as métissage: a means of weaving, producing, recreating and remining learning and teaching for a postdigital metaverse; a proposition that will be explored in Chapter 5.

References

Arndt, S., Bengtsen, S. S., Mika, C., & Nørgård, R. T. (2020). Spaces of life: Transgressions in conceptualising the world class university. In S. Rider, M. A. Peters, M. Hyvönen, & T. Besley (Eds.), *World class universities* (pp. 251–267). Springer.

Barnett, R. (1997). *Higher education: A critical business.* McGraw-Hill Education (UK).

Beckers, R., Van der Voordt, T., & Dewulf, G. (2015). A conceptual framework to identify spatial implications of new ways of learning in higher education. *Facilities, 33*(1/2), 2–19. https://doi.org/10.1108/F-02-2013-0013

Boden, T. A., Marland, G., & Andres, R. J. (2010). Global, regional, and national fossil-fuel CO2 emissions. *Carbon Dioxide Information Analysis Center, Oak Ridge National Laboratory, US Department of Energy, Oak Ridge, Tenn., USA Doi, 10.*

Brookfield, S. (1985). Self-directed learning: A critical review of research. In S. Brookfield (Ed.), *Self-directed learning: From theory to practice.* Jossey-Bass.

Carvalho, T., & Diogo, S. (2021). Time and academic multitasking – Unbounded relation between professional and personal time. In F. Vostal (Ed.), *Inquiring into academic timescapes* (pp. 137–155). Emerald Publishing Limited. https://doi.org/10.1108/978-1-78973-911-420211013

Chick, N. L., Haynie, A., & Gurung, R. (2011). *Exploring more signature pedagogies: Approaches to teaching disciplinary habits of mind.* Stylus Publishing.

Davids, N. (2021). Academic freedom and the fallacy of a post-truth era. *Educational Philosophy and Theory, 53*(11), 1183–1193. https://doi.org/10.1080/00131857.2021.1917363

Dewey, J. (1938). *Experience and education.* Kappa Delta Pi.

Freire, P. (1972). *Pedagogy of the oppressed.* Penguin Books.

Freire, P. (1974). *Education: The* practice of freedom. Writers and Readers Co-operative.

Gutiérrez, K. D., Baquedano-López, P., & Tejeda, C. (1999). Rethinking diversity: Hybridity and hybrid language practices in the third space. *Mind, Culture, and Activity,* 6(4), 286–303.

Hodson, M. (2021). *Climate scepticism, doomism and denial* [Paper presentation]. William Temple Foundation, July.

Hudson-Smith, A. (2022). Incoming metaverses: Digital mirrors for urban planning. *Urban Planning,* 7(2), 343–354. https://doi.org/10.17645/up.v7i2.5193

Husserl, E. (1907/1964). *The idea of phenomenology.* Nijhoff.

Kitto, S., Nordquist, J., Peller, J., Grant, R., & Reeves, S. (2013). The disconnections between space, place and learning in interprofessional education: An overview of key issues. *Journal of Interprofessional Care, 27*(sup2), 5–8.

Lukes, S. (1973). *Individualism.* Blackwell.

Mezirow, J. (1981). A critical theory of adult learning and education. *Adult Education, 32*(1), 3–24.

Nordquist, J., Sundberg, K., Kitto, S., Ygge, J., & Reeves, S. (2013). Future learning environments: The advent of a "spatial turn"? *Journal of Interprofessional Care,* 27(sup2), 77–81.

Nordquist, J., Sundberg, K., & Laing, A. (2016). Aligning physical learning spaces with the curriculum: AMEE guide no. 107. *Medical Teacher, 38*(8), 755–768.

Poyade, M., Rea, P., & Livingstone, D. (2019). Enhancing the curriculum in medicine, veterinary and life sciences using emerging technologies. *University Industry Innovation Magazine, 2019*(2), 20–21.

Savin-Baden, M. (2000). *Problem-based learning in higher education: Untold stories: Untold stories*. McGraw-Hill Education (UK).

Savin-Baden, M. (2008). *Learning spaces: Creating opportunities for knowledge creation in academic life*. McGraw-Hill Education.

Savin-Baden, M. (2023). *Digital and postdigital learning for changing universities*. Routledge.

Shulman, L. S. (2005). Signature pedagogies in the professions. *Dedalus Summer, 134*(3), 52–59.

Temple, P. (2008). Learning spaces in higher education: An under-researched topic. *London Review of Education*, *6*(3), 229–241.

Thomas, H. (2010). Learning spaces, learning environments and the dis 'placement' of learning. *British Journal of Educational Technology*, *41*(3), 502–511.

White, D. S., & Le Cornu, A. (2011). Visitors and residents: A new typology for online engagement. *First Monday*, *16*(9). https://doi.org/10.5210/fm.v16i9.3171

White, D. S., & Le Cornu, A. (2017). Using 'Visitors and Residents' to visualise digital practices. *First Monday*, *22*(8). https://firstmonday.org/ojs/index.php/fm/article/view/7802/6515#:~:text=In%20effect%2C%20the%20Visitors%20and,practices%20visible%20to%20each%20other

5

Tech, Platforms and Wearables in the Postdigital Metaverse

Introduction

This chapter begins by exploring the context of learning in the metaverse for a postdigital age. The postdigital is a term that is seen as both confusing and controversial, but it is a useful concept for explaining the impact of the digital on human and non-human actors. The second section of the chapter examines the tech and the platforms. Whilst some of these have been in use since the 1990s, many of these remain in use 25 years later, but there are now newer and more flexible options available. The final section presents new practices such as wearable devices and lifelogging.

The Postdigital

In this text, the postdigital is seen as a stance which merges the old and the new, it is not seen as an event or temporal position; rather it is a critical perspective, a philosophy, that can be summarized as a collection of stances. The postdigital is defined here as a stance towards the digital which seeks to challenge the educational, economic and ethical impact of digital technology on humanity and the environment. For example, whilst learning at universities through digital technology in the past has been seen as largely supplemental, it now takes centre stage. Whilst this shift was beginning to occur in 2019, the COVID-19 pandemic resulted in a realization that the digital was not separate from, but central to, learning in universities. Despite this shift, there remains little critical debate about the impact of the digital in terms of the economic impact of algorithms, ethical questions such as the use of i-slaves and surveillance undermining privacy. The postdigital might be perceived by some authors as just signalling a period of change (Fuller & Jandrić, 2019); here it is seen as a liminal and disruptive space in which to

DOI: 10.1201/9781003413875-6

untangle the impact of the digital on diverse systems (economic, sociological, political and ethical) and relationships. This chapter therefore sees the postdigital as a critical perspective, a philosophy, that can be summarized as a collection of stances which include:

- A disenchantment with current information systems;
- An exploration of digital cultures that is both still digital and beyond digital;
- The blurred and messy relationship between humanism and posthumanism;
- The condition of the world after computerization;
- The state of global networking and its development and;
- The expansion of the digital market.

Since the growth of the use of the term postdigital in around 2018, when there was a desire to try to define it as a term and a practice, the ground has shifted. The following section suggests the way the postdigital might be viewed in the next decade.

White (2009) argued that the postdigital was not about 'the new' bit, but rather about broader sociocultural questions such as the need to examine the impact on those who have no access to economic, social and political power. This neoliberal stance highlights the belief in competitive individualism and the growth of the market. Critics of neoliberalism (e.g. Giroux, 2005) suggest that the focus on economic outcomes results in unhelpful social, political and cultural biases for educational activities. Furthermore, Giroux and Giroux (2004) have argued that educators should build courses by combining 'democratic principles, values, and practices with… the histories and struggles of those often marginalized because of race, class, gender, disability, or age' (p. 99). They argue that academics should shift beyond the lands of academia and integrate with the larger spheres in the community, where culture and politics are truly learned and made relevant. However, perceptions of the postdigital differ across subjects and disciplines as exemplified in Table 5.1.

Some authors in the 2020s would argue that we are no longer in the postdigital (e.g. Cramer, 2015). The original drive to position the postdigital was probably in the late 1990s. Such positioning stemmed from the necessity of considering the impact of the (new/er) technologies on existing conceptions of posthumanism, artificial intelligence (AI) and the digital. It could be suggested that the drive for the postdigital began following the argument by Negroponte (1998) that the digital revolution was over. However, Taffel (2016) asserted that following Negroponte's digital revolution period, internet traffic increased as did global users, suggesting that the digital revolution continued beyond 1998. Yet early uses of the term postdigital were also

TABLE 5.1 Perceptions of the Postdigital Across Subjects and Disciplines (Savin-Baden, 2023)

Subject/Discipline	Explanation	Example
Quantum computing	The use of quantum bits to be in more than one state at a time, enabling the possibility of parallel calculation.	Carmody (2010)
Art	Artwork that points to flaws in digital processes, rather than seeking perfection.	Cascone (2000)
Architecture	Architecture which necessarily combines and acknowledges the synthesis between the virtual and the real, as well as the biological.	Spiller (2009)
Performance art	Creating body modifications.	Crawford (2012)
Geography	Exploration of contemporary urban spaces and cities as Code/Spaces.	Kitchin and Dodge (2014)
Education	Taking a stance against oppressive forms of education and encouraging learning through critical pedagogy.	Giroux (2005)
Postgraduate learning for healthcare professionals	Recognition that instead of standardized learning, the promises of technology can be redeemed through pedagogical approaches that create sufficient space and agency for students to engage.	Aitken (2021)
Postdigital storytelling	An argument for metamodernism deemed to be a new form of creative modality, where the divide between the digital and the non-digital is no longer in opposition, no longer binary.	Jordan (2019)

used to stand against a binary stance towards the digital, suggesting instead it should be seen not as an either other but as a continuum. For example, Pepperell and Punt (2000) suggested:

> The term Postdigital is intended to acknowledge the current state of technology whilst rejecting the conceptual shift implied in the 'digital revolution' – a shift apparently as abrupt as the 'on/off' 'zero/one' logic of the machines now pervading our daily lives. (p. 2)

Learning in the Postdigital Metaverse

Critical pedagogy is central to learning in the postdigital metaverse. Critical pedagogy, based on the work of authors such as Freire (1972), Mezirow (1985) and Giroux (1992), is a stance in which it is recognized that social and historical forces shape the processes through which people come to know themselves and develop their view of the world. Learning is therefore seen to occur in a social and cultural context, and this necessarily influences what and how people learn. Learners therefore must seek to transcend the constraints their world places upon them in order to liberate themselves and become critically aware.

> That most of our problems are human-created is both a cause for optimism and depression. Many problems could be addressed if people chose to do so. Yet a sense of inevitability – that nothing can be done – pervades our culture. Fast rhetorics are manifestations of a culture that suffers from attention deficit disorder, a culture where things are quickly used and discarded, a culture where the abuse of the environment and gaping inequalities are ignored. As Jackie Royster puts it, we need better ways of being and better ways of doing. We need pedagogies that encourage students to develop a sense of place, a sense of stewardship, a sense of equity, and a sense of connectedness to the world around them. We need to make better arguments about the value of slow rhetoric and be more imaginative about creating spaces where slow rhetoric can be practiced. The fate of future generations will depend on how well the students we teach can use slow rhetoric.
>
> **(Faigley, 2006, p. 9)**

At a time when the public good is under attack and there seems to be a growing apathy towards the social contract or any other civic-minded investment in public values and the larger common good, education has to be seen as more than a credential or a pathway to a job, and pedagogy as more than teaching to the test. Pedagogy is neither just a set of strategies and skills nor just a technique or method. Pedagogy should be something that brings to the fore relationships between knowledge, authority and power. Following Giroux (2016) pedagogy should raise questions, such as

- What knowledge is of most worth?
- What does it mean to know something?
- How can critical reflection be used to bridge the gap between learning and everyday life?
- How can the idea that pedagogy is not about receiving knowledge but transforming it be promoted?
- In what ways can students be enabled to explore the relationship between knowledge and power.

A postdigital stance towards critical pedagogy would also deconstruct the impact of capitalist digitization on learning. This form of critical pedagogy is not just about utopian values and critical hope, but instead suggests action which focusses on open debate, participatory pedagogies and openly distributed media. The drive for the postdigital therefore has developed from a need to critique the stances of the digital age and to deconstruct the language of capitalism, efficient algorithms and managed learning environments. This is reflected in some of the new and emerging perspectives on the postdigital.

The Tech and the Platforms

Whilst there are some obvious advantages to moving some teaching and learning into online spaces to address challenges of timetabling, limitations of classroom spaces and the time-consuming nature of commuting to campus, it is important that pedagogical reasoning underpins such decisions. Unfortunately, the experience of many students during the COVID-19 pandemic was of enforced online learning, and this pragmatic reasoning may have contributed to an ongoing assumption that online teaching and learning is a compromise rather than a reasoned decision. Many students did not consider their online learning experiences to be effective during this period (Ubell, 2022), and such negative concerns with online learning need to be addressed. Furthermore, tutors have been found to have negative perceptions of and resistance to online education, with aspects such as interpersonal challenges and limited time for training being cited as barriers to its adoption (Lloyd et al., 2012), as well as concerns about remaining technologically proficient in a rapidly changing technological environment (Richter & Schuessler, 2019). However, it is argued that where tutors have experience of online teaching, they perceive fewer barriers (Lloyd et al., 2012), perhaps indicating that their initial perceptions had been affected by apprehension of the tech and the platforms. It is possible that negative concerns held by tutors have reduced significantly in recent times as they have become accustomed to a wider range of technologies in post-pandemic education.

It is important at this stage to delineate some of the terminology that we use in this chapter as there are inconsistencies within the wider literature which can cause some confusion. We refer to technologies such as Moodle, Aula and Blackboard as learning management systems (LMS), which McGill and Klobas (2009) suggest 'process, store and disseminate educational material and support administration and communication associated with teaching and learning' (p. 496). As such, they are the online spaces where students can find module guides, assessment guidance, assignment submission links and general communications. In contrast, we refer to platforms as the dynamic online spaces used as virtual classrooms, where students connect, interact and learn. In asynchronous learning, the distinction between LMS and online learning platforms may be less apparent, as asynchronous discussion forums are a common feature of most LMS. However, in synchronous online learning, the students interact within virtual classrooms on platforms such as Microsoft Teams or Zoom.

Platforms in Context

Since the creation of learning platforms in the 1990s, they have, in the main, been considered to be a good thing. Universities such as Coventry University led the way in the United Kingdom at least in the use of virtual learning environments (VLEs) such as WebCT (which was then taken over by Blackboard). In the hands of creative staff developers early uses were innovative and focussed on pedagogically designed online learning. However, practices have changed, and the use of such platforms has become increasingly linear and overmanaged. The subtext of control is evident in many VLEs, not only through semiotics, symbols and terminology but also in the way learning is ordered in ways that suggest how teaching and learning should be in a neoliberal world. As Cousin (2005) has pointed out, these VLEs were fraught with images that are deeply problematic, such as 'a little white male professor' that adorned WebCT as its premier logo (p. 121). These images of scaffolding, structure and safety suggested stability and control. These systems still encourage staff not only to manage knowledge but also to manage discussions and possibly even to think and teach in linear ways. Clearly, in such striated spaces, both staff and students are 'being' positioned. There are further difficulties with the language of online learning. The notion of 'moderating' clearly locates the control with the lecturers. The notion of 'lurking' implies that silence and watching are inherently bad.

In areas such as problem-based learning there have been academics who have railed against this linearity. A number of PBLonline programmes and modules have been developed in order to provide support for students beyond the classroom. These programmes and modules use a problem-based learning approach but in online settings and focus specifically on enabling students to learning effectively in online teams. For example, Ronteltap (2006) and te Winkel et al. (2006) created innovative new learning spaces for students and developed new bespoke VLEs at the request of students on PBLonline modules. More recent examples include the development of PBLonline for Turkish distance education (Gunduz et al., 2016), speech and language students in Hong Kong (Ng et al., 2014) and medicine in the United States (Coiado et al., 2020).

Furthermore, with the growth of Massively Open Online Courses (MOOCs) and the evolution of global learning platforms, the ability to challenge the way learning occurs in online spaces has become increasingly difficult. Yet MOOCs have also commercialized and commodified learning. Whilst the rhetoric for MOOCs is to provide open and flexible learning that is 'free,' the presence of companies who are in the market for selling knowledge through them indicates that it is far from free. Such digital platforms administer knowledge rather than provide critical spaces for learning. The result is a growing deception of what learning is. The assumption is that learning:

- Can be contained through clearly defined content, detailed lesson plans and managed discussions;
- Should be managed in terms of time and content which is specified through narrow curricula focus and behavioural objectives;
- Should be structured in particular ways, often defined by timetables rather than pedagogy;
- Has boundaries, should not be creative and should not stray away from what has been defined in the module outlines and;
- Is not a social practice; the notion of social discussion in learning forums is invariably seen as 'interruptions' and such interruptions are often closed down by tutors.

This containment of learning is deception. It encourages students to see learning as content to be covered and the assessment as merely something to be passed. This deception began in the 1980s, with the development of modular systems and the use of behavioural objectives, which has resulted in knowledge being chunked and outcomes and assessment becoming the focus of all teaching. Such systems have not only undermined learning but indeed the purpose and function of the university. Moreover, since the 1980s, the situation has become more problematic, with relatively little critique of the systems adopted. Instead of staff being allowed to think about how learning should be enacted for 21st-century students, they seem to be continually expected to undertake administrative responsibilities imposed upon them. This ranges from managing the latest managed learning system and creating reusable lectures but also work such as 'inputting marks onto the system,' a task which could easily be undertaken by administrative staff. The work of the academic is no longer that of a researcher, thinker and creative teacher, but rather more of an administrator of managed knowledge.

Learning on the Platforms

Whilst a number of platforms have already been mentioned, this section offers an overview of the most used and useful platforms, along with research and reflections on their value for learning.

Zoom

Zoom is one of the most well-known webinar platforms. Its popularity increased during the COVID-19 pandemic, not only in education settings, but also amongst communities who had to work and socialize from home. In the 2020s, people became familiar with its features, resulting in it being one of the most downloaded apps of 2020 (Koetsier, 2021). It is straightforward to navigate and was the platform of choice for many higher education institutions (Elmer et al., 2021). Thus, Finatto Canabarro et al. (2023) conceptualize students' experiences of the sudden shift to online learning on Zoom as the creation of 'Zoom beings' (p. 7). However, there were a number of institutions who chose to ban its use due to a few instances of hacking. This is exemplified by 'Zoombombing' where meetings were disrupted by uninvited guests who had gained access to the online spaces due to its 'startlingly weak privacy and security protocols' (Elmer et al., 2021, p. 1), as well as the then UK Prime Minister Boris Johnson inadvertently revealing his personal Zoom meeting ID. Zoom has a clear and practical application for learning in the metaverse and has integrated collaborative tools and a useful breakout room function. Nevertheless, staff should ensure the security settings of their virtual classroom through randomly generated meeting links and password protection.

Teams

Microsoft Teams is used across higher education as a platform for meetings and as an application for file storage, and this familiarity makes it a useful platform for teaching and learning. Furthermore, as many universities provide students with Microsoft applications as part of their package of teaching and learning, it is often both accessible and familiar for students. This makes it a popular choice for online learning, and students report it to be a motivating and engaging online environment for synchronous learning (Rojabi et al., 2022).

As with Zoom, Teams includes integrated apps that can be used to encourage student collaboration and engagement, such as whiteboards, sticky notes features and Miro boards, and these can be used both in the main meeting room and in breakout rooms. As Teams can also be used to store documents, it is possible to create a Teams tile where the online learning sessions are hosted, and all associated collaborative documents are stored. This allows students to find everything in one space which can be useful whilst they gain confidence and competence in using new technologies. A further feature of sessions set-up within a tile is that the students can be divided further into team-specific channels. This allows multiple meeting, chat and storage spaces, where privacy settings can be applied in such a way that individual teams are only able to access their own work. The Teams app can be downloaded to mobile phones, allowing students to use the chat functions easily, thus encouraging interactions between sessions.

BigBlueButton

BigBlueButton is so called as its developers wanted its set-up to be as simple as pressing a big blue button (BigBlueButton, 2021). Indeed, it is commended for being relatively straightforward to use, and for its interoperability with LMS such as Aula, SmartClass and, in particular, Moodle (Ukoha, 2021). BigBlueButton is a useful platform for online learning as it allows the tutor to oversee multiple breakout rooms simultaneously. Tutors can join each of the breakout rooms with audio, and this opens a new browser tab for each one. They are then able to listen to teams' conversations one at a time whilst viewing them or can create a grid on their screen to view multiple teams simultaneously. BigBlueButton has an effective shared notes feature that allows students to collaborate on and view one document that they can download when required.

Engageli

Engageli has been developed as an online collaborative classroom space that attempts to replicate physical classrooms by using virtual tables in its online space. Students join a table when they log into the session, and instead of having to move in and out of breakout rooms, the facilitator changes the 'mode' of the session from room mode to table mode to alternate between conversations being class-wide or table-specific. Whilst some platforms have a function which enables the possibility of muting all participants, in Engageli, tutors can also click to request that all participants turn their cameras and/or microphones on. As well as having collaborative features such as whiteboards, sticky notes and Miro boards, Engageli features a private notes section for each student and facilitator. Participants can create screenshots of any slides or shared whiteboards, which can then be added to their individual notes. What is most useful is that whilst they have the option to download their notes, they can continue to view them each time they log into the classroom. Tutors can use this notes section to keep a memo of key points made in discussions that they may wish to summarize or comment on later, or alternatively they can log into the online classroom before a session to write some preparatory notes. Engageli is a useful platform for online learning; however, in our experience, its increased range of features and choices of views can make it a little less intuitive to navigate when using for the first time. Therefore, tutors should undertake more detailed training for this platform, to ensure the online session runs smoothly.

Meta Horizon Workrooms

As the name suggests, Horizon Workrooms are aimed more towards workplaces where employees work and collaborate remotely, rather than towards education. It can be described as mixed reality as it brings together virtual reality (VR), where students use VR headsets to engage, and the web, where students can log into sessions via a video call, in the same way as they would with online classrooms. This space is more reflective of learning in the metaverse than Zoom, BigBlueButton and Engageli because of its use of augmented reality and headsets. Where students use headsets, their digital avatar is present in the meeting, and some headsets track the participants' movements and facial expressions, which are then portrayed in the session (Hedrick et al., 2022). Other headsets do not have this function, leaving the avatar with what is affectionately referred to as a 'resting virtual bitch face.' Harfouche and Nakhle (2020) assert that using VR headsets give students confidence to engage thereby ensuring increased collaboration. Where students log in via the web, they then appear within the meeting on a virtual screen. Like Engageli, students in a Horizon Workrooms can break out to work on separate tables within the same space, working on their own whiteboard. Interestingly, although their own team's discussions within their hearing will predominate, all students will also hear some minimal background noise from other teams working, which may create a more authentic experience. The key difference between using VR classrooms instead of other online classrooms is the depth of experience that is added due to the sense of presence and proximity that arises from a three-dimensional interaction. Predictably, the barrier is the cost of technology if students are to engage using the VR headsets, such as the Meta Quest Pro or Meta Quest 2, as these are costly.

New and Emerging Technologies

The speed of technological change is resulting in the introduction of software, platforms and wearables at a faster rate than most higher education institutions can oversee and administer. Students are invariably more aware of the latest trends and innovations and therefore learning in the metaverse needs to be a space where staff and students are co-learners. This section outlines technologies such as the echoborg, which although not new is still underused and unfamiliar to many tutors in the higher education sector. More recent innovations such as wearable devices and adaptions are more likely to be seen as quirky and not part of what learning 'should be.' However, wearable devices, adaptions and life logging are likely to become part of the higher education landscape in the next five years.

The Echoborg

An echoborg is the use of a person to speak the words of an AI. A study by Corti and Gillespie (2016) created situations in which people conversed with an echoborg. In a series of three studies, the authors noticed that, unlike those who engaged with a text interface, the vast majority of participants who engaged with an echoborg did not sense any robotic interaction.

Corti and Gillespie (2016) suggest that whilst some studies have demonstrated that echoborgs may be perceived to be more intelligent and emotionally capable than bots, they do not know of any work that connects these interaction effects with technology acceptance. A more recent study by Stein et al. (2020) introduced participants to digital agents with varying embodiment (text interface/human rendering) and mental capacity (simple algorithms/complex AI). The results indicated that an agent based on simple algorithms only evoked discomfort when embedded in a human-like body; the AI being was always perceived as being uncannily eerie, regardless of its embodiment.

A recent fringe event occurred at the House of Lords All-Party Parliamentary Group on Artificial Intelligence entitled 'I am Echoborg!' which had first been staged as a television show before COVID-19. The fringe event was presented as a participatory Zoom show that invited the AI fringe group not to debate the future relationship of humans and intelligent machines in the abstract, but to discuss it with an AI. In the show, the AI speaks through an echoborg. It is programmed to recruit more echoborgs. Participating humans have to decide whether to become echoborgs or persuade the AI to agree to a different partnership. One of the participants in the fringe meeting argued that the echoborg was reminiscent of *The Matrix* (Wachowski & Wachowski, 1999). This film is the story of the fall of humankind, and the creation of AI that resulted in self-aware machines that imprisoned humanity in the Matrix, a VR system. Another person suggested that in some way the echoborg was not much more effective than ELIZA, the early natural language processing system that used pattern language, and which illustrated the illusion of understanding on the part of the programme, but which had no framework for contextualizing people or events.

Wearable Devices and Adaptions

In the late 1990s and early 2000s, ideas about postdigital humans related to the enhancement of humans. For example, in 1998, a set of experiments undertaken by Kevin Warwick, known as Project Cyborg, began with an implant into his arm used to control doors, lights and heaters. Later, this was developed into an implant inserted into his median nerve meaning his nervous system could be connected to the internet. In 2007, the performance artist Stelarc had a cell-cultivated ear surgically attached to his left arm and in a number of performances he allowed his body to be controlled remotely by electronic muscle stimulators connected to the internet. Herzogenrath (2000) argues that bodies are always in states of becoming, so the work of

TABLE 5.2 Classification of Active Implant Technologies (Clarysse, 2023)

Context	Invasiveness – Is the Implant Connected to the Brain or the Nervous System?	Implant Category	Example
Therapeutic health care	No	Therapeutic device	Pacemaker
	Yes	Therapeutic interface	Cochlear implant
Preventive health care	No	Preventive device	Biotelemetric electronic pill
	Yes	Preventive interface	Intracranial pressure monitoring sensor
Human enhancement	No	Insideable device	Radio Frequency Identification (RFID) microchip implant for contactless payment
	Yes	Insideable interface	Brain chip that lets user control computers by thought

Stelarc illustrates becoming through the process of forming assemblages with both other human and nonhuman bodies, in which (post)digital flesh is created.

More recently, interest in anthropotechnics, a term developed by Sloterdijk (2014), has been mounting. This is the idea of improving oneself and the world, through the adaption of the human body by combining technology with humanity. An example of this is recent work by Martijn Clarysse, at Ghent University, who has examined ways of extending the limits of the body and how people see and accept implants. Technologies which are used both inside and outside the context of healthcare are discussed, as well as implants with different degrees of invasiveness to the human body. Clarysse (2023) discusses how different types of technological implants are capable of extending the capabilities made possible by the human body and suggests they might be classified as shown in Table 5.2.

Other work in this area is in the exploration of the use of the brain to control a robotic arm (Edelman et al., 2019) and the use of a computer brain interface to generate images of what humans are thinking (Rosso, 2020).

Human Enhancement for Learning

To date, there is relatively little research which has explored, in depth, the use of human enhancement specifically for learning. A review article by Grewal et al. (2020) examined how human enhancement technologies affected customer experience in retail and service settings, many of which they suggest could be used and adopted in other disciplines. Many of the debates about human enhancement focus on ethics as well as discussions about how enhancement will enable or even ensure transhumanism. Transhumanism is a stance in which it is argued that technology can be used to transcend the limitations of the human condition. Authors such as Cohen and Spector (2020) suggest an extreme version of transhumanism which seeks to dispense with the body by transferring, or uploading, the human mind from the biological brain to a computer. This, they suggest, could facilitate travel within the solar system and enable galactic travel.

Lifelogging

Lifelogging is the use of technology to enable people to reflect and report on their everyday lives. Devices used include GPS tracking, wearable cameras, wearable sensors, such as heart rate monitors, and galvanic skin response sensors that measure changes in arousal. The value of life logging for learning in the metaverse is that it promotes reflection; something which is increasingly lost in the postdigital age. Whilst there are many types and delineations of reflection (see e.g. Savin-Baden, 2008) the concept perhaps most useful to the idea of lifelogging is 'reflection in action.' This, according to Schön (1983), is a form of conversation with a situation that is stimulated by complex problems not easily solved by trial and error. Thus, in the course of reflecting on a situation, we are holding a conversation between the task and our own mental understanding of that task. In a world where being fast and reactive is the norm, using lifelogging to promote reflective learning practices, whether in digital learning, spaces or face-to-face in the classroom, is vital for effective learning.

Conclusion

This chapter began by exploring the concept of the postdigital and the importance of this to learning in the metaverse. It then examined the current use of platforms, which, in the main, still promote linearity in learning, and which lack any real inventive avenues that may promote innovative learning practices for the metaverse. It is suggested that wearable devices and adaptations are currently underused in universities and that wearable devices in particular are likely to be adopted by students, even if they are not embraced by the mainstream university sector. Although the current focus in many universities in 2024 is the management of AI technologies such as ChatGPT and Claude.ai, more attention needs to be paid to wearable devices and human enhancement. Such new practices will bring advantages and challenges which will be discussed in Chapter 6.

References

Aitken, G. (2021). A postdigital exploration of online postgraduate learning in healthcare professionals: A horizontal conception. *Postdigital Science and Education, 3*(1), 181–197.

BigBlueButton. (2021). *Why is this project called BigBlueButton.* https://docs.bigbluebutton.org/support/faq.html#why-is-this-project-called-bigbluebutton

Carmody, T. (2010). *Embracing uncertainty: Making quantum computing work.* Wired. www.wired.com/gadgetlab/2010/11/embracing-uncertainty-how-to-make-quantum-computing-work/

Cascone, K. (2000). The aesthetics of failure: "Post-digital" tendencies in contemporary computer music. *Computer Music Journal, 24*(4), 12–18.

Clarysse, M. (2023). Extending the limits of the human body. Acceptance of implant technologies. In M. E. Mogseth & F. H. Nilsen (Eds.), *The limits of life.* https://www.berghahnbooks.com/title/MogsethLimits

Cohen, E., & Spector, S. (2020). Transhumanism and cosmic travel. *Tourism Recreation Research, 45*(2), 176–184.

Coiado, O. C., Yodh, J., Galvez, R., & Ahmad, K. (2020). How COVID-19 transformed problem-based learning at Carle Illinois College of Medicine. *Medical Science Educator, 30*(4), 1353–1354. https://doi.org/10.1007/s40670-020-01063-3

Corti, K., & Gillespie, A. (2016). Co-constructing intersubjectivity with artificial conversational agents: People are more likely to initiate repairs of misunderstandings with agents represented as human. *Computers in Human Behavior, 58,* 431–442.

Cousin, G. (2005). Learning from cyberspace. In R. Land & S. Bayne (Eds.), *Education in Cyberspace* (pp. 117–129). RoutledgeFalmer.

Cramer, F. (2015). What is 'Post-digital'? In D. M. Berry & Dieter, M. (Eds.), *Postdigital aesthetics* (pp. 12–26). Palgrave Macmillan. https://doi.org/10.1057/9781137437204_2

Crawford, A. (2012). Stelarc. *Art Monthly Australia, 248,* 10–11.

Edelman, B. J., Meng, J., Suma, D., Zurn, C., Nagarajan, E., Baxter, B. S., Cline, C. C., & He, B. (2019). Noninvasive neuroimaging enhances continuous neural tracking for robotic device control. *Science Robotics, 4*(31), eaaw6844. https://doi.org/10.1126/scirobotics.aaw6844

Elmer, G., Neville, S. J., Burton, A., & Ward-Kimola, S. (2021). Zoombombing during a global pandemic. *Social Media and Society, 7*(3). https://doi.org/10.1177/20563051211035356

Faigley, L. (2006). Rhetorics fast and slow. In P. Bizzell (Ed.), *Rhetorical agendas: Political, ethical, spiritual* (pp. 3–9). Lawrence Erlbaum Associates.

Finatto Canabarro, A. P., van der Westhuizen, A., Zanni, F., Abbadi, A., Shabnab, S., & Mölsted Alvesson, H. (2023). "We were like Zoom beings": Insider perspectives on student learning during the initial shift to online classes in Sweden at the outbreak of the COVID-19 pandemic. *Cogent Education, 10*(1). https://doi.org/10.1080/2331186X.2022.2160116

Freire, P. (1972). *Pedagogy of the oppressed.* Penguin books.

Fuller, S., & Jandrić, P. (2019). The postdigital human: Making the history of the future. *Postdigital Science and Education, 1*(1), 190–217.

Giroux, H. (1992). *Border crossings.* Routledge.

Giroux, H. A. (2005). The terror of neoliberalism: Rethinking the significance of cultural politics. *College Literature, 32*(1), 1–19.

Giroux, H. A. (2016). Beyond pedagogies of repression. *Monthly Review, 67*(10), 57.

Giroux, H. A., & Giroux, S. S. (2004). *Take back higher education: Race, youth, and the crisis of democracy in the post-civil rights era*. Macmillan.

Grewal, D., Kroschke, M., Mende, M., Roggeveen, A. L., & Scott, M. L. (2020). Frontline cyborgs at your service: How human enhancement technologies affect customer experiences in retail, sales, and service settings, *Journal of Interactive Marketing, 51*, 9–25, https://doi.org/10.1016/j.intmar.2020.03.001

Gunduz, A. Y., Alemdag, E., Yasar, S., & Erdem, M. (2016). Design of a problem-based online learning environment and evaluation of its effectiveness. *Turkish Online Journal of Educational Technology, 15*(3), 49–57.

Harfouche, A. L., & Nakhle, F. (2020). Creating bioethics distance learning through virtual reality. *Trends in Biotechnology, 38*(11), 1187–1192. https://doi.org/10.1016/j.tibtech.2020.05.005

Hedrick, E., Harper, M., Oliver, E., & Hatch, D. (2022). *Teaching & learning in virtual reality: Metaverse classroom exploration*. Intermountain Engineering, Technology and Computing. https://doi.org/10.1109/IETC54973.2022.9796765

Herzogenrath, B. (2000). The question concerning humanity. *Enculturation, 3*(1).

Jordan, S. (2019). *Postdigital storytelling: Poetics, praxis, research*. Routledge.

Kitchin, R., & Dodge, M. (2014). *Code/space: Software and everyday life*. MIT Press.

Koetsier, J. (2021, January 7). *Here Are the 10 Most Downloaded Apps of 2020*. https://www.forbes.com/sites/johnkoetsier/2021/01/07/here-are-the-10-most-downloaded-apps-of-2020/

Lloyd, S. A., Byrne, M. M., & Mccoy, T. S. (2012). Faculty-perceived barriers of online education. *Journal of Online Learning and Teaching, 8*(1).

McGill, T. J., & Klobas, J. E. (2009). A task-technology fit view of learning management system impact. *Computers and Education, 52*(2), 496–508. https://doi.org/10.1016/j.compedu.2008.10.002

Mezirow, J. (1985). A critical theory of self-directed learning. *New Directions for Continuing Education, 25*, 17–30.

Negroponte, N. (1998). *Beyond digital*. Wired. https://web.media.mit.edu/~nicholas/Wired/WIRED6-12.html

Ng, M. L., Bridges, S., Law, S. P., & Whitehill, T. (2014). Designing, implementing and evaluating an online problem-based learning (PBL) environment-a pilot study. *Clinical Linguistics and Phonetics, 28*(1–2), 117–130. https://doi.org/10.3109/02699206.2013.807879

Pepperell, R., & Punt, M. (2000). *The postdigital membrane: Imagination, technology and desire*. Intellect Books.

Richter, S. L., & Schuessler, J. B. (2019). Nursing faculty experiences and perceptions of online teaching: A descriptive summary. *Teaching and Learning in Nursing, 14*(1), 26–29. https://doi.org/10.1016/j.teln.2018.09.004

Rojabi, A. R., Setiawan, S., Munir, A., Purwati, O., & Widyastuti (2022). The camera-on or camera-off, is it a dilemma? Sparking engagement, motivation, and autonomy through Microsoft Teams videoconferencing. *International Journal of Emerging Technologies in Learning, 17*(11), 174–189. https://doi.org/10.3991/ijet.v17i11.29061

Ronteltap, F. (2006). Tools to empower problem-based learning: A principled and empirical approach to the design of problem-based learning online. In M. Savin-Baden & K. Wilkie (Eds.), *Problem-based learning online* (1st ed.). OUP/McGraw-Hill Education.

Rosso, C. (2020, November 27). New brain-computer interface transforms thoughts to images. *Psychology Today*. https://www.psychologytoday.com/gb/blog/the-future-brain/202009/new-brain-computer-interface-transforms-thoughts-images

Savin-Baden, M. (2008). *Learning spaces: Creating opportunities for knowledge creation in academic life*. McGraw-Hill Education.

Savin-Baden, M. (2023). *Digital and postdigital learning for changing universities*. Routledge.

Schön, D. A. (1983). *The reflective practitioner: How professionals think in action*. Basic Books.

Sloterdijk, P. (2014). *You must change your life*. John Wiley & Sons.

Spiller, N. (2009). Plectic architecture: Towards a theory of the post-digital in architecture. *Technoetic Arts*, 7(2), 95–104.

Stein, J.-P., Appel, M., Jost, A., & Ohler, P. (2020). Matter over mind? How the acceptance of digital entities depends on their appearance, mental prowess, and the interaction between both. *International Journal of Human-Computer Studies*, *142*, 102463.

Taffel, S. (2016). Perspectives on the postdigital: Beyond rhetorics of progress and novelty. *Convergence*, *22*(3), 324–338.

te Winkel, W., Rikers, R., & Schmidt, H. (2006). Digital support for a constructivistic approach to education: The case of a problem-based psychology curriculum. In M. Savin-Baden & K. Wilkie (Eds.), *EBOOK: Problem-based learning online* (1st ed.). McGraw-Hill Education (UK).

Ubell, R. (2022). *Staying online: How to navigate digital higher education*. Routledge. https://doi.org/10.4324/9781003036326

Ukoha, C. (2021). As simple as pressing a button? A review of the literature on BigBlueButton. *Procedia Computer Science*, *197*, 503–511. https://doi.org/10.1016/j.procs.2021.12.167

Wachowski, A., & Wachowski, L. (Directors). (1999). *The* Matrix [Film]. Warner Home Video.

White, D. (2009). *Postdigital: Escaping the Kingdom of the New*. https://daveowhite.com/postdigital-escaping-the-kingdom-of-the-new/

6

Pros and Cons of Learning in the Metaverse

Introduction

Learning in the metaverse is challenging for many staff in higher education. As mentioned in Chapter 1, what counts as the metaverse and how learning is to be managed within it still remain troublesome. This chapter examines a number of advantages of learning in the metaverse such as the opportunity to be inclusive towards different approaches to learning, the value of affordances, peer-to-peer learning and genres of participation. The second section of the chapter explores some of the challenges of learning in the metaverse. These challenges include digital inequalities and surveillance, the question of virtue ethics, power and control, and mis/placed digital identities.

Pros of Learning in the Metaverse

Whilst there are concerns raised by many academics about the impact of the metaverse on learning, we would argue that the benefits outweigh the challenges. However, it is clear that the progress in the use of digital media for learning following the COVID-19 pandemic appears to have regressed in universities rather than continued to develop. Certainly, research during and after the pandemic indicated that students, worldwide, valued the university approaches adopted in online spaces (Savin-Baden, 2024). Some of the advantages are as follows.

Support for Diverse Approaches to Learning

With the growth of neoliberalism across the university sector, the metaverse offers the opportunity to move away from values that require teaching and learning in narrow and particular ways. One such opportunity, which fits well with the metaverse, is that of critical pedagogy. Critical pedagogy, based on the work of authors such as Freire (1972) and Mezirow (1985), as

DOI: 10.1201/9781003413875-7

mentioned in Chapter 2, and more recently Giroux (1992; 2016), is a stance that recognizes that social and historical forces shape the processes through which people come to know themselves and develop their view of the world. Learning is therefore seen to occur in a social and cultural context, and this necessarily influences what and how people learn. Learners therefore must seek to transcend the constraints their world places upon them in order to liberate themselves and become critically aware. At a time when the public good is under attack and there seems to be a growing apathy towards the social contract or any other civic-minded investment in public values and the larger common good, education has to be seen as more than a credential or a pathway to a job, and pedagogy as more than teaching to the test. Pedagogy is neither just a set of strategies and skills nor just a technique or method. Pedagogy should be something that brings to the fore relationships between knowledge, authority and power. Central to this kind of pedagogy is an understanding of the value of the digital and the impact that particular affordances have on learning.

Valued Affordances

The concept of affordances has become increasingly used in research and technology since the late 1980s. The term originated from Gibson (1979), who developed the ecological approach to visual perception in which he argued that: 'When no constraints are put in the visuals system, we look around, walk up to something interesting and move around it so as to see it from all sides, and go from one vista to another. That is natural vision …' Thus, it is possible to see how this term has been (mis-)appropriated when we realize that he argued: 'The *affordances* of the environment are what it offers, the animal, what it *provides* or *furnishes*, for good or ill' (p. 115, original italics). The use then of 'affordances' seems at one level to have provoked an overemphasis on what particular technologies prompt or allow us to do, bringing with it a sense of covert control. On the other hand, there is a sense that the term is used because it offers a linguistic position and format through which it is possible to discuss the complexity, interactions and impact of technologies on higher education. The notion of agency of objects centres on the argument that digital devices mediate social relations and that they are implicated in the formation of human subjects (Ruppert et al., 2013). Yet this idea seems to imply that humans lack agency and have little choice in the ways in which they operate or little ability to critique the media put before them.

However, as Ruppert et al. (2013) argue, there is a need to explore *how* digital devices themselves are materially implicated in the production and performance of contemporary sociality. The authors suggest that there is a need to rethink the theoretical assumptions of social science methods, because they believe that a return to an older, observational kind of knowledge economy, based on the political power of the visualization and mapping of administratively derived data about whole populations is occurring. At the same time, there is a need to examine the ways in which observation is 'being performed by the digital and its material and productive effects' (p. 11). Yet government surveillance and the monitoring of our shopping habits have been taking place for many years; it is the sophistication that has changed. However, we propose that this focus by Ruppert et al. (2013) is too narrow, and instead we suggest the notion of tethered integrity is important here (Savin-Baden, 2015). Tethered integrity captures the idea that many of those who are always on, who are digitally tethered, do in fact have a degree of integrity about their use of social networking sites. Whilst some studies indicate that youth have more integrity in this area than adults (Brandtzæg et al., 2010) there is also an increased recognition of the power of such sites to manipulate what is shared, what is bought and the ways in which people behave. At the same time, it is important to acknowledge that technologies such as augmented reality (AR) have distinct affordances, such as

a. The ability to blend real and digital environments.
b. Enabling the application of AR for exploring real-world sites such as the Virtual Skiddaw project created by Daden, a virtual field trip using the Unity3D game engine (https://www.daden.co.uk/_files/ugd/0c2908_e9c87a3bee0342dd8a26a2aabd129df1.pdf?index=true).
c. Creating digital artefacts collaboratively that can be shared and reused, such as peer projects at Birmingham City University, UK Innovation Fest (https://www.innovationfest.co.uk/).

Peer-to-Peer

Peer-to-peer learning is generally talked about in relation to group learning in schools and universities. The focus is on sharing, supporting and guiding one another as part of a learning team. Tutor-guided learning teams are the most common form of group learning seen in schools and universities. The tutor in this type of team sees his or her role as guiding the students through each component of the problem or challenge, and thus the students see the problem as being set within or bounded by a discrete subject or disciplinary area. In some situations, the tutor actually provides hints and tips on problem-solving techniques; the argument for such an approach is that students have limited skills to help them solve the problems they will encounter. The result is that students often see solutions as being linked to specific curriculum content. However, in an extensive meta-analysis that included hundreds of studies, Johnson (1991) concluded that collaborative learning arrangements were superior to competitive, individualistic structures on a variety of outcomes such as higher academic achievement, higher-level reasoning, more frequent generation of new ideas and solutions and greater transfer of learning from one situation to another. The difference between cooperative learning and collaborative learning is that cooperative learning involves small group work to maximize student learning. This approach tends to maintain traditional lines of knowledge and authority, whereas collaborative learning is based on notions of social constructivism. As Matthews (1996) puts it 'it (collaborative learning) is a pedagogy that has at its centre the assumption that people make meaning together and that the process enriches and enlarges them' (p. 101). It is this kind of collaborative learning that is increasingly being used by young people creating, producing and making together through social networking and practices such as vidding. However, students tend to move away from formal peer-to-peer learning at school when not required to do so, in order to ensure they understand the work for themselves and gain the grades they seek. Yet often peer-to-peer learning occurs informally in the metaverse, particularly in gaming communities such as *Space Invaders* and *Minecraft*.

Informal peer-to-peer learning is defined here as learning that is based on learning through interaction with peers that is not *required* by parents or a teacher, although the interaction may occur as a result of school work. In this form of learning, young people help, encourage and challenge each other through informal peer support. This may occur face to face by doing homework together on the school bus but is more likely to occur through informal media groups such as sharing through WhatsApp or texting one another in real-time whilst doing homework. What is important in this learning is that it is peer-led, as Ito et al. (2010) argue:

> Peer-based learning relies on a context of reciprocity, in which kids feel they have a stake in self-expression as well as a stake in evaluating and giving feedback to one another. Unlike in more hierarchical and authoritative relations, both parties are constantly contributing and evaluating one another. (p. 22)

Our digitized, globalized society continues to offer young people a range of mixed messages, and one which remains deeply troublesome is the relationship between individual and peer learning. Lukes (1973) coined the term the 'ethic of individualism.' The ethic of individualism here depicts the notion that some students saw learning within the group as an activity that was only valuable in terms of what they as an individual could gain from it (Lukes, 1973). This is still pertinent now. The focus remains on grades of individual achievement at school and university. At the same time, students are expected to develop an interactional stance. Interactional stance captures the way in which a learner interacts with others within a learning situation. It refers to the relationships between students within groups, and staff-student relationships at both an individual and a group level.

Interactional stance encompasses the way in which students interpret the way they as individuals, and others with whom they learn, construct meaning in relation to one another (Savin-Baden, 2000). It may be characterized also by the individual placing him/herself at the centre of the value system. Learning within the group is seen as an activity that is only valuable in terms of personal gain for the individual, but there have been shifts away from such stances in digital spaces, with moves towards more informal peer learning and participation.

Genres of Participation

Ito et al. (2010) argue that the studies they undertook focussed on cultural and social categories, rather than the particular variables such as age, gender and class, examined by other researchers. For example, they avoided categories such as technoboys and computer-competent girls (Holloway & Valentine, 2003) or traditionalists and specialists (Livingstone, 2002). Instead, Ito et al. (2010) argue for genres of participation with media, which they define as a 'constellation of characteristics' which are constantly changing. The three genres are as follows:

Hanging Out

Young people in the study by Ito et al. (2010) expressed a desire to hang out, to be independent of parents, families and intuitional structures. Hanging out involved fluid movement between online and offline activities, and what was noticeable was that young people spent considerable time organizing and discussing the process and possibilities for hanging out, as well as actually 'doing' the hanging out. Young people used media to facilitate hanging out through instant messaging, texting and Facebook to arrange face-to-face meetings, as well as to share their tastes such as music, by posting posters, pictures and sharing music on social networking sites. What is interesting about current practices is the layering that occurs so that young people would hang out together in the same room but could be involved in different and possibly overlapping activities such as playing an online game, texting others and making food. Thus, teenagers were constantly in touch with one another online, offline and face-to-face, sharing spaces together.

Messing Around

This was characterized by teenagers being involved in intense exploration and engagement with new media, rather than being particularly friendship driven, involving both 'looking around' and 'experimentation and play':

> Looking around online and fortuitous searching can be a self-directed activity that provides young people with a sense of agency, often exhibited in a discourse that they are 'self-taught' as a result of engaging in these strategies ... The autonomy to pursue topics of personal interest through random searching and messing around generally assists and encourages young people to take greater ownership of their learning processes ... As with looking around, experimentation and play are central practices for young people messing around with new media. As a genre of participation, one of the important aspects of messing around is the media awareness that comes from the information derived from searching and, as we discuss in this section, the desire and (eventually) the ability to play around with media.
>
> **(Ito et al., 2010, p. 57)**

Messing around was seen as being easier to undertake for those teenagers with high-speed internet, private space, free time and autonomy, as well as the relevant gadgets to support their messing around. What was interesting in the study by Ito et al. was that, despite these advantages enjoyed by some, the most important spaces for messing around were in either school or after-school contexts, which shows the value of informal learning, the need for student-led exploration and the value of space and time to explore and experiment with or alongside others. Messing around is argued to be a transitional space for geeking around:

> Although messing around can be seen as a challenge to traditional ways of finding and sharing information, solving problems, or consuming media, it also represents a highly productive space for young people in which they can begin to explore specific interests and to connect with other people outside their local friendship groups.
>
> **(Ito et al., 2010, p. 65)**

Geeking Out

This is defined as intense engagement with technology or media exemplified through fandom or committed gaming but this was not always driven by technology. The kinds of activities seen in this genre varied from gaming to offline activities such as playing sports. One example of this would be a teenager spending time finding and producing information about gaming rules to share with others, so that they can all progress higher up an online game.

Geeking out was characterized by Expertise and Geek Cred, and rewriting the rules. Expertise and Geek Cred involved having high levels of complex knowledge in narrow domains, high-level expertise that was recognized and often employed by others to save time and resources. Rewriting the rules transcended geeking out and messing around, Ito et al. (2010) explain:

> … there are important differences in the ways in which the rules are rewritten in each of these genres of participation. Like messing around, which involves an inchoate awareness of the need and ability to subvert social rules set by parents and institutions such as school, geeking out frequently requires young people to negotiate restrictions on access to friends, spaces, or information to achieve the frequent and intense interaction with media and technology characteristic of geeking out. Rewriting the rules in the service of geeking out, however, also involves a willingness to challenge technological restrictions -to open the black box of technology, so to speak. This practice is most often done in the service of acquiring media … Geeking out often involves an explicit challenge to existing social and legal norms and technical restrictions. It is a subcultural identity that self-consciously plays by a different set of rules than mainstream society. (p. 71)

Table 6.1 summarizes this work and also suggests areas where boundary crossing is evident.

TABLE 6.1 Summary of Genres of Participation

Genre	Hanging Out	Messing Around	Geeking Out
	Being independent of parents, families and institutional structures and using new media to maintain online and offline connections with friends	Intense exploration and engagement with new media, but also used to explore specific interests and to connect with other people outside their local friendship groups	Intense engagement with technology or media characterized by fandom or committed gaming but is not always driven by technology
Boundary crossing	Peer Sociability ⟶	Interest driven messing around	
		Rewriting ⟵	⟶ rules
		e.g. Illegal downloading of songs to share with friends	e.g. Illegal video file sharing requiring high level subverting of rules
		Social play ⟵	Geeky interest driven activity
Focus	Construction of spaces for offline and online friendship drive activities	Open ended participation requiring time and resources	Highly social and engaged in terms of interest, but not expressed as being friendship driven
Type	Friendship driven	Transitional space: Friendship driven and Interest driven	Interest driven

Hanging out, messing around and geeking out all require time, space and resources to experiment with autonomy in ways that are self-directed. Genres of participation are not related to types of young people, but rather the diverse types of activities in which teenagers participate and engage – some do one; some all; some are more interest-driven than others.

Cons of Learning in the Metaverse

The challenges of learning in the metaverse are many and varied, and in particular emphasizes learning inequalities and issues of control that occur through the misplaced use of digital media, whether through face recognition software or other forms of surveillance.

Digital Inequalities and Surveillance

Digital inequalities are defined as those inequalities such as skills, use and access that affect people's ability to exploit technology to support their life chances, as well as to grow and learn (Savin-Baden, 2024). Digital inequalities are largely spread through relational technologies: knowledge and news are spread through tweets, memes, shares and likes. Social media, whether Twitter, Snapchat or TikTok, influence our lives, often in ways that are not realized. The result is that social opinion becomes knowledge. Thus, truth(s) are socially engineered by the prolific voices of social media because there are no restrictions on the socialization of digital technologies. The result is widening inequality – digital, social and political. Further layers of this are seen in the global increase in the invention of fake news; when state, military and political leadership prohibit or suppress social media usage, such as in China or North Korea; and in the West suppressing or hiding news coverage of legitimate demonstrations and miscarriages of justice.

The challenge about inequalities and hiding truth also introduces concepts concerning just how much surveillance is going on, especially in the metaverse if commercial companies have a free rein. One insight into what might develop comes from a recent book by Zuboff. In her book *The Age of Surveillance Capitalism: The Fight for a Human Future at the New Frontier of Power*, she argues that we have already entered a new and unprecedented era, that of surveillance capitalism, in which the dominance of the main technology companies, notably Google, Facebook, Apple and Amazon, has adapted capitalism to suit their own ends and over which the rest of us appear to have little or no control (Zuboff, 2019). In order to analyze this, she develops her own conceptuality. This form of capitalism is a new logic of accumulation, based upon the realization that the apparently useless extra data that is now available through the mechanisms by which the digital can track both our movements, desires and behaviours, and can produce a behavioural surplus, which is then turned into prediction products. The technology companies extract this data without our consent or consultation, so we become the raw material and not even the product of this process. By this means, companies can reduce the levels of uncertainty about our future preferences, be those to do with consumption or politics, and thus shape our behaviour towards guaranteed outcomes. Even though we may be aware of this, most of us seem content to trade off our privacy and the intrusion of such targeting for the supposed benefits of convenience and ease of communication. If this is then pursued further through various forms of the metaverse, there are some disturbing implications about the power of the few to determine the values incorporated into these new technologies.

Virtue Ethics

Virtue ethics is a broad term for theories that emphasize the role of character and virtue, rather than focussing on consequences or actions. The idea is that the focus is on someone displaying virtues and being humanitarian in a variety of contexts over time. However, the ability to cultivate the right virtues is affected by education, society, friends and family. Virtue ethics is usually defined as four types:

- Eudaimonist virtue ethics – eudaimonist versions of virtue ethics are that they define virtues in terms of their relationship to *eudaimonia*, translated as happiness or flourishing, and sometimes as well-being.
- Agent-based virtue ethics – these virtue ethicists argue that qualities should be explained in terms of the motivational and dispositional qualities of agents, such as rightness and wrongness.
- Target-centred virtue ethics – these virtue ethicists' views developed from their existing conceptions of the virtues. Examples of existing virtues include generosity, courage, self-discipline and compassion.
- Platonistic virtue ethics – Plato's dialogues seemed to devote time to asking his fellow Athenians to explain the nature of virtues like justice, courage, piety and wisdom (Chappell, 2014). What seems to be central to Platonist virtue ethics is the idea of contemplating goodness to create new habits and improve oneself.

The modest ethics approach rejects over-arching ethical frameworks, and their limited respect for the empirical complexities of real-world scenarios, and the power and agency that such frameworks ascribe to human rationality. Modest ethics instead embraces a deep interconnection between ethics and materiality, leading to a new kind of worldly ethics, which can be embraced within and across the metaverse. In practice, modest ethics in the context of the metaverse can help us recognize the impact we have on the environment.

Ethical frameworks are often constructed in order to cope with such complexity and produce criteria by which we can evaluate human action and make decisions about the right way forward. Modest ethics encourages us to become more comfortable with that which we cannot control, and which is constantly moving beyond us. Modest ethics may demand that we move more slowly and carefully, even within the fast-moving metaverse, rather than dashing ahead in ways that our culture and digital technology encourage us to do. What is needed then is a rethinking of pedagogy in virtuous and modest ways of creating learning communities that are valued in the metaverse.

Power and Control

There is a tendency for established and experienced members of staff to focus on covering content rather than finding new ways in which the metaverse can enable students to learn effectively. Yet approaches to teaching in the metaverse differ not only because of the medium being used but also because of issues of identity, presence and immersion that occur in that environment. This is because being in the metaverse prompts us and our students to engage with issues of embodiment and questions about positioning and power. For example, some questions that relate to these issues might include staff asking does it matter if:

- Students come to class as an animal?
- Students stand, dance or walk off in the middle of a discussion?
- Students come to class carrying a gun?
- Students change their clothes whilst the teacher is speaking?

Whilst at one level these questions might seem obvious and simplistic, they do raise questions about what learning might or should look like in the metaverse. It introduces questions about the role of staff and students in such spaces and issues relating to levels of engagement, and expectations of real-world behaviours.

Learning in higher education retains persistent patterns which are often exemplified in the relationships seen in discussion forums in a virtual learning environment, compared with dialogue and discussions in the metaverse. Power relationships tend to be blurred more in the metaverse between staff and students. For example, tutors' expectations and the priming of students to undertake assessments in particular ways were more apparent in the virtual learning environment discussion forum than in virtual worlds. Much of this could be attributed to the asynchronicity of the discussion forum and the way it was organized in a question-and-answer format. Perhaps the contained spaces of the discussion forum, rather than the more ungraspable spaces of virtual worlds, prevent students from determining both their 'academic destiny' and their own competence. Unilateral control would seem to be at odds with the metaverse, and thus it would seem the blurring of power relationships might enable a redistribution of educational power, so that components of the curriculum become spaces of consultation for students rather than those of containment and control. Yet metaverse spaces can also be ones where identities shift and change, not always in helpful ways.

Mis/placed Digital Identities

There is still a sense that place is seen as a more stable identity than space, although the polarity is perhaps less stark in 2025 when location finders, GPS systems and digital maps on mobile devices result in collisions of space and place. However, what is perhaps more of an issue here is identity tourism, a metaphor developed by Nakamura to portray identity appropriation in cyberspace, which has relevance to the metaverse. The advantage of such appropriation enables the possibility of playing with different identities without encountering the risk associated with racial and gender differences in real life. Yet:

> One of the dangers of identity tourism is that it takes this restriction across the axes of race/class in the 'real world' to an even more subtle and complex degree by reducing non white identity positions to part of a costume or masquerade to be used by curious vacationers in cyberspace.
>
> **(Nakamura, 2000)**

We travel through the metaverse putting on and taking off identities, as we cross fluctuating boundaries and bounce between our virtual and real-life worlds; and identity tourism offers opportunities to 'play away' from other identities. Yet staff have certainly questioned the extent to which metaverse identities have spilled over into work or home identities and affected or prompted reformulations of other identities in other worlds. This is illustrated in Table 6.2.

Sinclair refers to this sense of having a left-behind identity in relation to her disquiet about the relationship between her real-life and *Second Life* identity

TABLE 6.2 Identities in Flux (Savin-Baden, 2010, p. 75)

	Characteristics	Purpose or Function	Relationship with Other 'Identities'	Example
Identity tourism	Wholehearted appropriation of another identity	Playing away from other more responsible identities	Different and invariably subversive, often pernicious	Changing racial or sexual identity for deceitful purposes
Identity expansion	Several, but often the same voices in a wide range of spaces, a kind of expanded voice	To increase profile and voice across digital spaces	Similar, copied and stretched	The use of multiple blogs and websites
Identity multiplication	Different identities in diverse spaces	Identity exploration in different spaces and contexts	Different from one another but with a sense of coherence relating to real-life identities	Creating avatars in different virtual worlds and games
Changelings	Residual identity which has a sense of being a left behind identity	A denial of current other identities or a mirroring of real-life identities due to ambivalence about them	Either dislocated from other identities or strongly copied	Avatars that are used transgressively or are used as copies of other stronger identities
Shapeshifters	A transformation into a different form and persona	This is unclear but usually a choice related to solving a difficulty of some kind	Usually the same, it is the form that is usually different	Shift to another form such as animagi in *Harry Potter*, or characters in the film *X-Men*

(Savin-Baden & Sinclair, 2010). However, some scholars suggest that it is important to have a clear conceptual understanding of who we are in cyberspace, since without it we risk being confused (e.g. Floridi, 2011). Those like Floridi who argue for such a stance seem to suggest that by separating and being clear about identities brings with it some kind of honesty or morality, yet this would seem misplaced. Similarly, Kimmons and Veletsianos (2014) argue that the ability to undertake identity explorations relies on the

> user's ability to separate the legion of one's virtual, exploratory selves from the real life or traditionally viewed unitary self. In the Web 2.0 world, however, one's ability to do this diminishes as anonymity declines, real life connections are replicated in the virtual medium, web resources are used for surveillance, and sites like Facebook and LinkedIn seek to present 'authentic,' unitary selves that are similar to the selves expressed in real life. (p. 8)

Nevertheless, this stance would seem misplaced, since identity exploration does not require a clear separation of identities, but a recognition that identities are not just multiple and fluid but overlap and shift according to context. For example, recent work in this area suggests the need for a network formalization of identity theories. In practice, this means that there should be a drive to prevent centralized identities in order to counter the desire by governments and institutions to monopolize and control online identities (Rychwalska, 2023). Rychwalska (2023) suggests a new model that brings together identity theory and social identity theory and proposes architectural principles for decentralizing digital identities. Rychwalska (2023) argues that fluid online identities need to be recognized more readily since many such identities overlap, she suggests

> There is no need for a digital identity system to be able to publicly prove all meanings related to every identity; rather, it should facilitate relating those meanings to specific social contexts, where the alters provide verification of the identity. Thus digital identities should be required to allow a variety of different identities (from very private to very public) and identity verification fitted to the audience. Fulfilling these identity needs would make digital social spaces also meet the requirement of contextual integrity (Nissenbaum, 2004) – identities expressed within specific contexts would be restricted to these contexts and under the control of the individual. (p. 2088)

Thus, there needs to be a shift away from globally verifiable attributes towards more innovative flexible and fluid identity systems.

Conclusion

This chapter has examined a series of complex issues related to learning in the metaverse. It is clear that there are ethical concerns related to power, control, inequalities and identity. However, the exploration and research to date about student experiences of learning remain largely positive. New technologies that support learning are predominantly welcomed by students, but it is evident that institutions and staff need to embrace such technologies more readily. Future developments and new possibilities will be explored further in Chapter 7.

References

Brandtzæg, P. B., Lüders, M., & Skjetne, J. H. (2010). Too many Facebook "friends"? Content sharing and sociability versus the need for privacy in social network sites. *International Journal of Human–Computer Interaction, 26*(11–12), 1006–1030.

Chappell, T. (2014). *Knowing what to do: Imagination, virtue, and platonism in ethics*. OUP.
Floridi, L. (2011). The construction of personal identities online. *Minds and Machines, 21*(4), 477–479.
Freire, P. (1972). *Pedagogy of the oppressed*. Penguin Books.
Gibson, J. J. (1979). *The ecological approach to visual perception*. Houghton Mifflin.
Giroux, H. (1992). *Border crossings*. Routledge.
Giroux, H. A. (2016). Beyond pedagogies of repression. *Monthly Review, 67*(10), 57.
Holloway, S. L., & Valentine, G. (2003). *Cyberkids: Children in the information age*. Routledge Falmer.
Ito, M., Baumer, S., Bittanti, M., Boyd, D., Cody, R., Herr-Stephenson, B., Horst, H. A., Lange, P. G., Mahendran, D., & Martínez, K. Z. (2010). *Hanging out, messing around, and geeking out*. MIT Press Cambridge, MA.
Johnson, D. W. (1991). *Cooperative learning: Increasing college faculty instructional productivity. ASHE-ERIC higher education report no. 4, 1991*. ERIC.
Kimmons, R., & Veletsianos, G. (2014). The fragmented educator 2.0: Social networking sites, acceptable identity fragments, and the identity constellation. *Computers & Education, 72*, 292–301.
Livingstone, S. (2002). Young people and new media: Childhood and the changing media environment. Young people and new media (pp. 1–278). https://www.researchgate.net/publication/248492147_Young_People_and_New_Media
Lukes, S. (1973). *Individualism*. Blackwell.
Matthews, R. S. (1996). Collaborative learning: Creating knowledge with students. In R. H. Menges, & M. Weimer, & Associates (Eds.), *Teaching on solid ground: Using scholarship to improve practice* (pp. 101–124). Jossey-Bass.
Mezirow, J. (1985). A critical theory of self-directed learning. *New Directions for Continuing Education, 25*, 17–30.
Nakamura, L. (2000). *Race In/For Cyberspace: Identity Tourism and Racial Passing on the Internet*. https://smg.media.mit.edu/library/nakamura1995.html
Ruppert, E., Law, J., & Savage, M. (2013). Reassembling social science methods: The challenge of digital devices. *Theory, Culture & Society, 30*(4), 22–46.
Rychwalska, A. (2023). *"I am no number": Humanizing digital identities*. 56th Hawaii International Conference in System Sciences, 2081–2090. https://hdl.handle.net/10125/102456
Savin-Baden, M. (2000). *Problem-based learning in higher education: Untold stories: Untold stories*. McGraw-Hill Education (UK).
Savin-Baden, M. (2010). *A practical guide to using Second Life in higher education*. McGraw-Hill Education (UK).
Savin-Baden, M. (2015). *Rethinking learning in an age of digital fluency: Is being digitally tethered a new learning nexus?* Routledge.
Savin-Baden, M. (2024). *Digital and postdigital learning for changing universities*. Routledge.
Savin-Baden, M., & Sinclair, C. (2010). Lurking on the threshold: Being learners in silent spaces. In R. Land & S. Bayne (Eds.), *Digital difference* (pp. 29–44). Sense Publishers.
Zuboff, S. (2019). *The age of surveillance capitalism: The fight for a human future at the new frontier of power*. Profile Books.

7

Learning Assemblages for the Metaverse

Introduction

This chapter examines the idea of learning assemblages, which reflects changing views of how learning might be seen in the metaverse. It begins by presenting the notion of learning assemblages and illustrates why this is important to the metaverse. The chapter then explores issues that are related to the idea of assemblages, beginning with context and collision collapse, and digital métissage. The latter half of the chapter discusses ways of rethinking place, space and presence, suggesting that these concepts are currently defined too narrowly and need to be re-examined in light of future forms of learning in the metaverse.

Learning Assemblages

In the world of education where online learning, machines and people coalesce, there is often assumed to be a symmetry in the relationship between computers and people. Indeed, during the COVID-19 pandemic, people were constantly tethered to machines and reliant on them for communication with loved ones, shopping and sustaining their mental health. However, in the 2020s, learning assemblages have become more varied, as exemplified by the speed of change and shifts in teaching and assessment practices, as Goodyear (2022) argues

> The possibility and speed of change has highlighted the fragility of apparently engrained practices and revealed their dependence on expectations about social and technical arrangements that are no longer stable. (p. 35)

Learning assemblages then interrupt linear scaffolded forms of learning since they embrace ideas such as learning as folding and moving away from networks and scaffolding.

DOI: 10.1201/9781003413875-8

The boundaries between the human and the non-human as machines have become a blurred assemblage. The concept of assemblage used here is based on the work of Deleuze and Guattari (1988) which reflects the ideas of connection, transformation and becoming. Deleuze argued in conversation with Parnet (Deleuze & Parnet, 1987):

> What is an assemblage? It is a multiplicity which is made up of heterogeneous terms and which establishes liaisons, relations between them, across ages, sexes and reigns - different natures. Thus, the assemblage's only unity is that of a co-functioning; it is a symbiosis, a 'sympathy'. It is never filiations which are important, but alliances, alloys; these are not successions, lines of descent, but contagions, epidemics, the wind. (p. 69)

This is the kind of assemblage that needs to be central to learning in the metaverse. In recent years, there have been discussion about spaces becoming more blurred between the physical and the digital, an example of blurred assemblages is the phygital. This is the concept of using technology to bridge the digital world with the physical world with the purpose of providing a unique interactive experience for the user. This is not a term we find particularly useful in relation to the metaverse since it is rather simplistic in the face of changing contexts, notions of spatiality, new perspectives on place, space and presence and the growing importance of context and collision collapse.

Context and Collision Collapse

It is clear at the end of this text that many – whether business people, academics, companies or universities may assume that the impact of the metaverse will result in bigger visions and loftier learning spaces, but in many ways what we are really seeing is context collapse. The idea of context collapse was first suggested by boyd (2002) who argued:

> ... that the contextual information that they draw from does not have the same implications online. Situational context can be collapsed with ease, thereby exposing an individual in an out-of-context manner. (p. 12)

Whilst contexts may have collapsed, as boyd (2002) suggests, some years later it is evident that those using social networking sites do increasingly have a sense of their audience. Yet at the same time, the varied, mainstream and often linked social media sites are places and spaces that could be said to be resulting in multiple, though perhaps different forms of, context collapse. In practice, within the metaverse, this means that public and private identities may collapse in ways that have negative repercussions on learning. One such example is context collision where people link professional and personal accounts to project particular kinds of authenticity context collision. Davis and Jurgenson (2014) argue that context collapse can be divided into context collusion and context collision. Context collusion is the intentional collapsing of context, such as the use of social media to blur contexts, for example, the merging of public and private identities on Facebook. They explain:

> Context collusions are those in which users draw on the affordances of interaction platforms to bring together multiple networks, for varying purposes and to varying degrees. One might elicit sympathy through a Facebook status update, elicit consulting work via LinkedIn, information via Twitter, or funds via Kickstarter. Collusions are a combined product of platform design and user practice, as users intentionally transcend network boundaries. (p. 6)

Context collision is the unintentional collapsing of context, often resulting in the violation of privacy rules. In practice, this ensues when information transcends normal assumed boundaries. For example, collision occurred when Facebook made settings more open than users realized, or may arise when an employee posts comments about their superiors on Twitter.

Thus, in terms of the metaverse it is important to be clear about boundaries, better ethical practises and the rules of operation within the spaces where learning takes place. An example of this can be seen in gaming spaces, where ethical norms are interrupted and often collapse, illustrated by this discussion and reflection, Figure 7.1. The context is that a discussion began about theft in virtual worlds between a colleague, Dr. Maria Power, who is an ethicist, and I. The conversation is provided followed by a reflection from Zak Savin-Baden (2025).

Furthermore, with the growth of the metaverse, the notion of context collapse is even more poignant than in former years. Digital spaces collide with, change and recreate real-life spaces. The merging of the real and the digital is almost seamless. There is also the realization that these worlds collapse in on each other as new technologies shift and haptics become more sophisticated, resulting in the impression of us almost always being in liminal spaces; the result is a sense of provisionality. As contexts collapse across global spaces and within digital spaces the borders of everything become increasingly fluid and braided; a digital métissage.

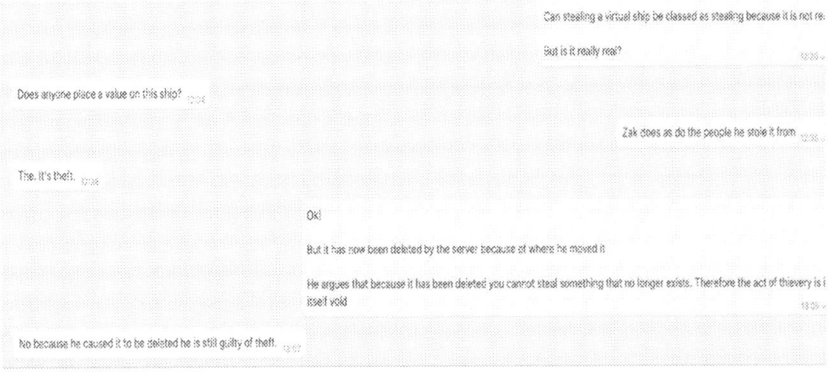

Can stealing a virtual ship be classed as stealing because it is not re

But is it really real?

Does anyone place a value on this ship?

Zak does as do the people he stole it from

The. It's theft.

Ok!

But it has now been deleted by the server because of where he moved it

He argues that because it has been deleted you cannot steal something that no longer exists. Therefore the act of thievery is i itself void

No because he caused it to be deleted he is still guilty of theft.

The above discussion follows the ethical conversation after a virtual spaceship was effectively stolen in the game Space Engineers and then with a subsequent abuse of Server Behaviour, the ship was then vanished. The logic being that because said ship no longer exists and was deleted by the server, no one is technically liable for its deletion or its theft. With the response being that because the ship had been given value both by its owners and the party committing the actions against said spacecraft, it still had value and therefore classed as theft. Further it is interesting because the laws of the real world often do not transcend into the virtual one, an example being that it is positively encouraged in various PvP games to kill the opposing side and this is not seen as murder. Applying this logic to the situation, a large grey area emerges since all Space Engineers Servers have rules which must be followed.

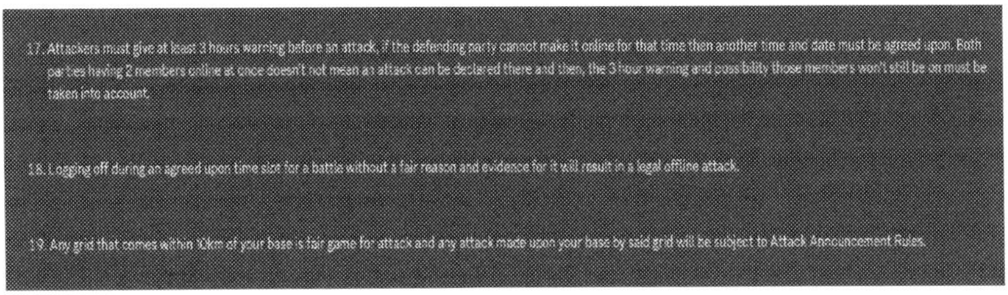

17. Attackers must give at least 3 hours warning before an attack, if the defending party cannot make it online for that time then another time and date must be agreed upon. Both parties having 2 members online at once doesn't not mean an attack can be declared there and then, the 3 hour warning and possibility those members won't still be on must be taken into account.

18. Logging off during an agreed upon time slot for a battle without a fair reason and evidence for it will result in a legal offline attack.

19. Any grid that comes within 10km of your base is fair game for attack and any attack made upon your base by said grid will be subject to Attack Announcement Rules.

Although the destruction/vanishing of a ship was caused, it was done without a single aggressive action and therefore it is highly debatable whether it would be considered an attack. Yet it still would be considered theft as discussed above. The idea of value certainly has various interesting affects within the virtual world. One question that could be asked is how much does that extend to affect the real world?

(Z. Savin-Baden, 2025)

FIGURE 7.1 Ethics collision.

Digital Métissage

Digital *métissage* captures the idea of blurring genres, texts, histories and stories in digital formats that recognize the value and spaces between and across cultures, generations and representational forms (Savin-Baden & Wimpenny, 2014). Meaning-making in the digital age means trajectories are not straightforward, and managing this digital *métissage* offers interesting, if challenging possibilities. The notion of métissage (French meaning hybridization or fusion) brings with it the sense of braiding, so that the process of digital métissage requires co-production and co-creation with participants in ways that braid data and stories. Digital métissage is based on the idea of literary métissage as outlined by Hasebe-Ludt (2009). Literary métissage is the process of creating stories that are braided together and rooted in history and memory, as well as being stories of becoming. The principle of métissage in terms of positioning learning is not easily located within the metaverse and prompts consideration of ways of working across boundaries in fluid ways. Yet engaging with digital métissage does challenge staff to request that students share their learning narratives in a way that prompts reflective learning when learning in new and different digital spaces. Co-creation is defined here (following Boydell, 2011; Saldaña, 2010) as a collective activity between participants, artists and researchers that attends to the processual aspects of participants' experiences. Using these forms of co-creation will enable those learning in the metaverse to create collaborative learning in ways that result in a co-created learning collective and encourage students to reconsider notions of place, space and presence.

Place and Space

Although the COVID-19 pandemic promoted new ways of seeing learning, it also raised questions and challenged assumptions about the value of physical co-presence and collaboration and how place and space might be re-viewed. Place is generally defined as a specific site or locale. Early work by Dawson et al. (2014) explored issues such as how territoriality and identity result in spaces with diverse understandings of legitimacy. This edited collection disrupts dominant narratives about space and draws attention to situations in which different social constructions of space and territory coincide, collide or overlap. More recently, studies of displacement stories begun to prompt reconsideration of the fixity of people and place (see, e.g. Butler-Kisber et al., 2023, an edited collection on stories of displacement).

Dealing with the complexity of the relationship between place and space has been the purview of geographers for many years. Indeed, Agnew (2011) has pointed out that the conflict between the dominant meanings of place in

TABLE 7.1 Dimensions of Place and the Metaverse

	Physical Space	Metaverse Space
Places as location	A space where an activity is located such as a skills laboratory.	A virtual laboratory in a virtual world used to practise skills.
Place as series of locales	University campus where social interaction takes place.	Created interactive spaces such as gaming environments or virtual world social spaces.
Place as a sense of place	Disciplinary space which is a unique community and landscape.	A disciplinary space in a virtual world created specifically for disciplines, for example, engineering, nurses, sociologists.

space is longstanding. However, Agnew offers some helpful dimensions of place: place as location, place as series of locales and, finally, place as a sense of place. Applying these definitions to the metaverse and the learning occurring within it illustrates the fluidity between notions of place and space as shown in Table 7.1.

Table 7.1 illustrates that place affects and is affected by space, particularly in the metaverse. This is because virtual places are often seen more as spaces because of their mutability, as Thrift has argued. For example, he suggests that place weaves together space and time and argues for the materiality of places as 'open spaces' that practices make and that take 'shape only in their passing' (Thrift, 1999, p. 310), and therefore places are necessarily time-space configurations. Yet it is also important to note, as White (2021) suggests, that the 'mistake is to assume that if we can see each other's bodies then we must be together in the same place.'

> Whether it's the location of topic areas in the library, the paragraphs in an essay, the bullet points in our notes or the way we arrange files on our computers, understanding (how we arrange and develop our thoughts) has a spatial element to it. Even the phrase 'making a connection' is inherently spatial. In a similar manner our social relations are spatial, from where we sit in a meeting to if we spend most of our time in the kitchen at parties. Both the social and the conceptual involve us creating schema and maps to navigate by.
>
> **(White, 2021)**

In a recent family discussion, we explored the idea that in the 21st century, it was probably impossible to find a place that was no longer digital. For example, a room has a digital temperature control, gardens have digital watering systems and even a mountain such as Mont Blanc becomes digital when someone climbing to the summit carries a mobile phone. So whilst all places could be argued to be digital not all such places create a sense of presence or a sense of being embodied or being in the digital space, as discussed in Chapter 1. However, the notion of presence in digital spaces needs to be reconsidered.

Presence

Lombard and Ditton explored the use of presence in the media and communication literature, which is work that now has resonance with learning in a digital age. They identified six ways of conceptualizing presence (Lombard & Ditton, 1997), which are summarized and adapted as follows:

Presence as social richness. This kind of presence is defined as the extent to which a medium is perceived as sociable, warm, sensitive, personal or intimate when it is used to interact with other people. Presence as social richness centres on the concepts of intimacy and immediacy.

Presence as realism. The second conceptualization of presence relates to the extent to which a medium can produce seemingly accurate representations of objects, events and people – representations that look, sound and/or feel like the real thing.

Presence as transportation. This form of presence is about the extent to which one is transported to another place in three ways: (a) the user is transported to another place, (b) another place and the objects within it are transported to the user and (c) where two (or more) communicators are transported together to a place that they share. The difficulty with this version of presence is that these distinctions are now somewhat obsolete in a virtual world such as *Second Life*, since virtual worlds can encompass all of these definitions.

Presence as immersion. Presence here is the idea that one experiences perceptual and psychological immersion. Whilst immersion has been central to discussions and explorations of virtual reality, immersion has only become of more interest in terms of virtual humans since the development and popularity of virtual worlds. Dede (1995) describes immersion within learning environments as the subjective impression that a user is participating in a 'world' comprehensive and realistic enough to induce the 'willing suspension of disbelief' (Coleridge, 1817).

Presence as social actor within medium. This is where people respond, compliment or experience anger towards characters in a television programme, computer game or virtual world as if they were communicating with real people. Whilst in the past this largely occurred in privacy in people's homes, this form of presence has expanded in diverse ways such as the development of *Gogglebox* (Lambert & Alexander, 2013). This UK television show uses a camera to watch people sitting in front of the television in their own homes, which also records their observations and reactions to the previous week's television, and this is then broadcast. Other forms of social commenting occur through people using apps such as TikTok to record and share their responses to films and television shows.

Presence as medium as social actor. This is where presence involves people's social responsiveness towards a medium itself, not characters within a medium, whereby the presence emerges from a medium's characteristics. This can be seen in gaming but also in the use of virtual performance. For example, Chafer and Childs deconstructed two scenes from *Hamlet* that were performed live in a recreation of the Globe Theatre in *Second Life* (Chafer & Childs, 2008; Kuksa & Childs, 2010).

It is clear from these definitions that what counts as presence has become increasingly complex with the changing landscape of the metaverse. The notion of presence in the past, the sense of being there physically, was, in general, associated with clear definitions and boundaries yet in the 21st-century presence transcends real and virtual spaces in fluid ways. For example, the notion of presence in learning has previously been focussed on the idea of education taking place; the sense of being there, drawn from Heidegger's (2000) notion of *dasein*. However, with the shift towards the digital and more recently the metaverse, there has been a move away from the idea of being there, to more of a sense of dwelling, a sense of becoming absorbed in and through the metaverse. Learning and education in the metaverse should be movement and dwelling held together loosely; in the space between building and dwelling (Sennett, 2018) where the focus is on community, conversation and improvisation. His argument is that built spaces, he suggests cities, but we would also suggest built campuses, stifle aspiration and are intent on order and control. Thus, in a postdigital age, as we live with fluid edges, building, dwelling in and beside the metaverse, there is a need to transcend our presence in research, teaching, home, hobbies and sports. Yet at the same time, we need to be aware of the impact of absent presence on learning and education within the metaverse.

Absent Presence

Absent presence in the 21st century is largely associated with the original work of Derrida (1997), who suggested that languages, images and ways of representation can help us to see that social media captures our presence. However, it is also seen as deriving from the point made by Socrates in Plato's *Phaedrus* (c. 370 BC; 2002), that the absence of the writer from a (circulated) text leaves it open to misinterpretation. Examples of this include the biblical letters sent to communities to explain Christ's teaching, such as the letter of James (*New International Version Bible*, 2015) which is seen to be controversial. More recent examples are the works of Charles Dickens which were sold as single chapters, such as *The Pickwick Papers* (Dickens, 1836) and the *Penny Dreadful*. This was a cheap, often sensationalist popular serial publication, with titles such as the *Vampire, The Feast of Blood* and *The Black Band*, produced during the 19th century in the United Kingdom; each costing one penny (Springhall, 1994). However, absent presence can also be seen in other ways, such as in the presence of onscreen personalities and events that can generate the illusion of almost immediate presence or even (particularly with television) parasocial interaction and the symbolic or actual deletion of a particular sociocultural group (e.g. women, LGBTIQA+ or ethnic minorities) in a text, genre or social context (Chandler & Munday, 2011).

The process of listening to social media, often presented from afar can result in the construction and deconstruction of our values and those with whom we share our lives every day. As Gergen (2009) notes, absent presence results in a shift from vertical to horizontal relationships. Vertical relationships are those which occur with significant others and are relationships that require time and commitment. Horizontal relationships are those which occur across the networks of cyberspace where there is little need to do more than 'like' a post or offer a short comment. Friendship in the horizontal sphere is therefore superficial. One of the perils of absent presence is the way in which particular activities or devices can result in inside and outside spaces. For example, as Gergen (2009) argues:

> Cell phone conversation typically establishes an 'inside space' ('we who are conversing') vs. an 'outside space' constituted by those within earshot but prevented from participating. The fact that 'it doesn't matter whether you listen or not' underscores the impotent insignificance of the outsider. (p. 238)

Thus, outside spaces such as this can result in resentment because of having to listen to a stranger's conversation on a train or by being an outsider to a conversation of a loved one with someone else. The need to respond all the time, even to posthumous posts suggests either that people control us (we have time to take the call) or that our time is more important and valuable than those we are with face-to-face (we take the call to show how precious our time is). We live in a world where the present and absent have an equivalent value.

Today, absent presence is a feature of all mediated communication, where people are separated from one another by time and space, yet the combination of chronic telepresence and absent presence is having a challenging impact on learning. Furthermore, absent presence in today's world of social media is invariably seen as something necessarily negative. Examples of negative absent presence might include:

- Double screening; families may choose to watch a film together as a shared event but in the process of doing this everyone is also on their phone at the same time.
- Students who are participating in a seminar may be partially listening to the lecturer whilst planning their social life on their phones with students in the same room.
- A couple go out for dinner to talk and catch up with one other but spend most of the time catching up with posts and friends on social media on their phones.

TABLE 7.2 Absence and Presence (Savin-Baden, 2023)

Description	Media Example	Higher Education Example
Present presence: talking to someone face-to-face.	Speaking face-to-face via Skype.	Participating in a seminar onsite.
Present absence: speaking to someone directly who is not with us.	Speaking to someone directly on the phone.	Engaging in a seminar online.
Absent presence: someone you are with is communicating with someone elsewhere.	You are talking to someone face-to-face, and they pull out their phone to post a message on Instagram.	Students being on social media during an onsite lecture.
Absent absence: complete absence of the person.	Messaging a dead person on Facebook.	Sharing images of deceased staff or students as a form of remembrance.

In the 21st century, these examples are familiar to most people. Yet there are other forms of absent presence that could be viewed in a more positive light. An example might be that of being absorbed in a play, piece of music or a rock climb, thus being with other people whilst also being deeply absorbed. The difference between this example and the negative ones is the lack of mobile phones, which, as Gergen (2009) has suggested, tends to subvert or reverse the impact of other communication technologies. Definitions of different types of absence and presence are suggested in Table 7.2.

Present Absence

Present absence became increasingly common during the COVID-19 pandemic when meeting and learning online became the norm, along with the associated headaches of spending too much time on screen. White also noted how meetings resulted in questions about our own embodiment in a sea of screen faces. This sense of being with and not being with others as well as seeing our own disembodied on-screen presence:

> ... a digital, synchronous doppelganger floating alongside images of people laminated onto a two dimensional surface like samples on a microscope slide. The result is a distressing panopticon where we are trapped under the omnigaze of all, while somehow not 'seeing' each other or feeling any meaningful presence.
>
> **White (2021)**

This, White suggests, has resulted in skeuomorphic presence; the idea that we are a copy of ourselves on a screen, and imitation. Yet such an imitation, a mirroring of ourselves, often seems to decrease our sense of presence and embodiment.

Reflection and Conclusion

Learning and education in the metaverse offer opportunities to re-examine and possibly reconstruct our disciplinary and institutional pedagogies. Such opportunities might occur by examining conceptions of learning and teaching, by shifting from notions of generalizable learning styles to identity-located learning stances, as mentioned in Chapter 4, and by embracing the idea of spatial ecology in the context of higher education. Spatial ecology is defined here as the creation of balance between and across spaces in higher education, so that account is taken of not merely knowledge, content, conceptions and acquisition but also of ontology, values and beliefs, uncertainty and complexity. The idea of spatial ecology captures the idea that it is recognized that staff and students operate on diverse trajectories and when they collide new learning spaces in the metaverse emerge and often unexpected learning occurs. For example, differences in staff and students' stances towards particular concepts such as family, climate change, oppression and gender within a virtual world prompt staff and students to consider the diverse spaces in which they live, work and learn and the impact of their life-world on their learning. It is through discussion and exploration that notions of translation, shifting spaces and spaces of representation along with diverse and difficult territorial positions, are recognized. Yet in order to create innovative and challenging metaverse spaces, it is important to realize that a tentative learning balance exists between confusion and transformation. As learners and teachers, we are not apolitical, acultural or disembodied beings, but we are often disturbed and uncomfortable; it is important that we have a sense of how our presuppositions affect and have an impact on those with whom we interact in the metaverse.

This chapter has explored the impact of a number of interruptions on learning and life. The boundaries between places and spaces, the digital and non-digital have collapsed and collided resulting in changes whose impact we are as yet to comprehend fully. Furthermore, the relationship between absence and presence has also shifted, bringing with it an increasingly and constant sense of skeuomorphic presence. The metaverse is shifting learning spaces whether in education or business, into new spatial ecologies many of which we are yet to understand.

References

Agnew, J. (2011). Space and place. In J. Agnew & D. N. Livingstone (Eds.), *The sage handbook of geographical knowledge* (pp. 316–331). Sage.

boyd, d. (2002). *Faceted ID/entity: Managing representation in a digital world* [Master's thesis]. Massachusetts Institute of Technology.

Boydell, K. M. (2011). Making sense of collective events: The co-creation of a research-based dance. *Forum: Qualitative Social Research, 12*(1). https://www.qualitative-research.net/index.php/fqs/article/view/1525/3143

Butler-Kisber, L., Clark, K., & Savin-Baden, M. (2023). *Narrative inquiry of displacement: Stories of challenge, change and resilience*. Taylor & Francis.

Chafer, J., & Childs, M. (2008). The impact of the characteristics of a virtual environment on performance: Concepts, constraints and complications. *Learning in Virtual Environments International Conference*, 20–21 November 2008, The Open University, UK P94-10, 94.

Chandler, D., & Munday, R. (2011). *A dictionary of media and communication*. OUP Oxford.

Coleridge, S. T. (1817). *Biographia literaria* (J. Engell & W. Jackson Bate, Eds.). Princeton University Press (Printed 1983, Vol. 1).

Davis, J. L., & Jurgenson, N. (2014). Context collapse: Theorizing context collusions and collisions. *Information, Communication & Society, 17*(4), 476–485. https://doi.org/10.1080/1369118X.2014.888458

Dawson, A. C., Zanotti, L., & Vaccaro, I. (2014). *Negotiating territoriality: Spatial dialogues between state and tradition*. Routledge.

Dede, C. (1995). The evolution of constructivist learning environments: Immersion in distributed, virtual worlds. *Educational Technology, 35*(5), 46–52.

Deleuze, G., & Guattari, F. (1988). *A thousand plateaus: Capitalism and schizophrenia*. Bloomsbury Publishing.

Deleuze, G., & Parnet, C. (1987). *Dialogues* (H. Tomlinson & B. Habberjam, Trans.). Columbia University Press.

Derrida, J. (1997). *Of grammatology* (G. Spivak, Trans.). Johns Hopkins University Press.

Dickens, C. (1836). *The Pickwick papers*. Chapman & Hall.

Gergen, K. J. (2009). The challenge of absent presence. In *Perpetual contact* (pp. 227–241). Cambridge University Press. https://doi.org/10.1017/cbo9780511489471.018

Goodyear, P. (2022). Realising the good university: Social innovation, care, design justice and educational infrastructure. *Postdigital Science and Education, 4*(1), 33–56.

Hasebe-Ludt, E. (2009). Writing lives, writing worlds: Literacy as autobiographical and cosmopolitan text. In *Challenges bequeathed: Taking up the challenges of Dwayne Huebner* (Vol. 46). (pp. 25–37). Brill.

Heidegger, M. (2000). *Being and time* (J. Macquarrie & E. Robinson, Trans.). Blackwell.

Kuksa, I., & Childs, M. (2010). But a walking shadow: Designing, performing and learning on the virtual stage. *Learning, Media and Technology, 35*(3), 275–291.

Lambert, S., & Alexander, T. (2013). *Gogglebox*. Channel 4. https://www.channel4.com/programmes/gogglebox

Lombard, M., & Ditton, T. (1997). At the heart of it all: The concept of presence. *Journal of Computer-Mediated Communication, 3*(2), JCMC321.

New International Version Bible. (2015). Hodder & Stoughton. https://www.biblegateway.com/versions/New-International-Version-NIV-Bible/

Plato. (2002). *Phaedrus* (R. Waterfield, Trans.). Oxford University Press.

Saldaña, J. (2010). Writing ethnodrama: A sampler from educational research. In M. Savin-Baden & C. H. Major (Eds.), *New approaches to qualitative research: Wisdom and uncertainty* (pp. 77–85). Routledge.

Savin-Baden, M. (2023). *Digital and postdigital learning for changing universities*. Routledge.

Savin-Baden, Z. (2025). Fighting a just war in a digital realm. In M. Power & M. Savin-Baden (Eds.), *Artificial intelligence and just war theory*. CRC Press.

Savin-Baden, M., & Wimpenny, K. (2014). A practical guide to arts-related research. In *A practical guide to arts-related research*. Brill.

Sennett, R. (2018). *Building and dwelling: Ethics for the city*. Farrar, Straus and Giroux.

Springhall, J. (1994). Disseminating impure literature: The 'Penny Dreadful' publishing business since 1860. *Economic History Review, 47*(3), 567–584.

Thrift, N. (1999). Steps to an ecology of place. In Massey D, J. Allen, & P. Sarre (Eds.), *Human geography today* (pp. 295–323).

White, D. (2021, February 1). *Spatial collaboration: How to escape the webcam*. Blog. https://daveowhite.com/2021/02/

Index

Note: *Italic* page numbers refer to *figures* and **Bold** page numbers refer to **tables**

I

J

K

L

M

N

O

Printed in the United States
by Baker & Taylor Publisher Services